A Rabbi
LOOKS AT THE
LAST DAYS

Rabbi Jonathan Bernis

JVMI
PUBLISHING

Fourth Printing

JVMI
PUBLISHING

a division of:

Jewish Voice
Ministries International

Jewish Voice Ministries International
P.O. Box 31998
Phoenix, Arizona 85046-1998
Phone: 602.971.8501
Fax: 602.971.6486
Toll Free 24 hour order line: 1-800-306-0157

Preface

A great event is taking place in this world of ours, and almost nobody seems to notice.

It amazes me that even Christian authors who are focused on the Last Days do not recognize what is taking place in the Jewish community around the world.

Just as the Bible predicted, the Jewish People are being restored to their Land and to their Messiah. Not in some far distant End Times — but right now!

Although Jewish people who accept *Yeshua HaMashiach* (Jesus the Messiah) are often ostracized by their families, friends, and business associates, Jews all over the world are turning to Him and becoming Messianic Jews in numbers not seen since the first century.

I am weary of reading the dogmatic positions expressed in much apocalyptic literature. Some authors will tell you with absolute confidence that they know exactly when and where the significant events of eschatology are to take place. Yet, in most instances, they ignore what is truly significant.

Perhaps the saddest reality of all is that predominant eschatological positions today frequently impede efforts by evangelical believers to reach Jewish people with the Gospel... and discount the relevance of doing so.

So, I have written this book in juxtaposition to much else that is *out there* on the subject of the Last Days. Like the little mirror on the right side of your car suggests, *objects in your mirror are closer than you think.*

I hope you enjoy reading this book. In fact, if you do, please tell a friend about it.

Acknowledgements

As surely as I begin to thank everybody who has contributed to this book, I am going to leave someone out. At the risk of doing so, however, I want to single out some extra-special people who have been instrumental in getting this book to press.

My precious bride, Elisangela, and my little princess, daughter Li'el, have graciously given up some of *our* time in order to get this on paper. They have never failed to greet me with wide-eyed enthusiasm when I do show up — an excitement that is punctuated with those most special of all words, "Papai's home!" They are the loves of my life.

It all really began for me with Ernie and Maria Beck who helped me find my Messiah and who have consistently modeled godly character for more than twenty years. To you two, I am deeply indebted for a firm foundation.

I would be remiss if I did not wrap my arms tightly around the staff of Jewish Voice Ministries International. The faithful execution of their tasks during this writing discipline made it possible for me to devote the time necessary to complete the work, knowing full well that they would be *faithful to the end.*

Special thanks to Sherri Wyner for her graphic design of the cover of the book and her relentless pursuit of excellence in editing the manuscript.

Wayne and Bonnie Wilks of the Messianic Jewish Bible Institute, who are partners in ministry with us, have been a constant source of personal encouragement. They continue to partner faithfully in pursuit of the Gospel, to the Jew first and then to the rest of the world.

Finally, thanks to Dave Wimbish, for his help with the manuscript.

And for all those other faithful companions whose names should have been included here for your gracious financial and prayer support, I am eternally grateful.

And most of all, thanks and praise to my beloved *Yeshua HaMashiach* for redeeming my life.

Table of Contents

Part One

"... AND THEN THE END WILL COME"

Chapter One

WHAT IF EVERYTHING YOU'VE BEEN TOLD ABOUT THE LAST DAYS IS WRONG?

The mark of the beast... Gog and Magog... 666... a confederation of ten nations... the antichrist's ascendancy to power... the abomination of desolation...

The Bible says that all of these are signs that the end of the world is near (or at least the end of the world as we know it).

Over the past few years, many Christians have become obsessed with trying to unravel the Bible's mysterious prophecies about such things. When they read the daily newspaper or watch the news on television, they analyze every word to see if there might be a connection to the End Times. This is especially true if that news has to do with Israel or the Middle East.

And yet, while we focus on such esoteric matters, other more obvious signs that the End Times are upon us are happening right in front of our eyes — and we don't seem to notice.

What if much of what you've been told about the End Times is wrong, or at the very least off target? What if you've been looking for the signs of Messiah's return in all the wrong places?

Before we go any further, let me explain that there's nothing wrong with seeking to understand Bible prophecies and live in the light of that understanding. This is precisely what God expects us to do. I'm not writing this book to say, "Stop trying to understand the Book of Revelation," or anything of the sort. It's just that we mustn't be so focused on things like red heifers and saber-rattling in the Middle East that we miss out on the marvelous thing God is doing right now to prepare the world for the Messiah's return.

Who am I?

You may be wondering why I'm qualified to write this book. Let me tell you a little bit about who I am:

- A Jew by birth.
- A Messianic Rabbi with degrees in Theology, Jewish Studies and Early Christianity.
- A Messianic Rabbi who has established and led a number of Messianic Jewish congregations, both in the United States and abroad.
- A follower of Messiah in active ministry for more than 28 years.

- The President of Jewish Voice Ministries International, an organization that reaches out with physical and spiritual help and hope to Jewish People all over the world.

I hold dual citizenship in the United States and Israel and frequently lead teaching tours to the Holy Land. I have done extensive post-graduate study in archaeology, including work at archaeological excavation sites in Israel. I have an understanding of Israeli history that is deepened by personal experience.

I grew up in Rochester, New York, in a traditional Jewish family. We always went to synagogue for the High Holy Days, and celebrated Passover, Chanukah, and the other significant Jewish feasts. I attended classes at the synagogue and had a bar-mitzvah (Jewish rite of passage for males) at 13, but had no real desire to serve God with my life.

A holy change in plans

I knew I had a head for business, and my plan was to get a degree in business and make as much money as possible as quickly as possible. God, however, had other ideas.

In high school, a wrestling coach I admired was a committed follower of Jesus. It intrigued me to hear him talk about his faith. For the first time in my life, I thought of Jesus as someone other than the son of Mr. and Mrs. Christ, the one who had done so much harm to the Jewish People.

But still, I had always been taught that I was born a Jew and would die a Jew, and that Jews did not believe in Jesus.

Jesus was not an option for me.

After high school, I went off to the University of Buffalo to major in business. It was there that I began experimenting with drugs, eastern meditation, and the occult.

By the grace of God, my drug use never got completely out of hand. That was not true of a young woman I knew who was almost destroyed by drugs. She quit going to class. She stopped caring about her appearance. Every time I saw her, she looked worse than before — her eyes bloodshot, her hands shaky, and her hair unkempt. I tried several times to help her, although I didn't really know what to do except to be her friend.

Finally, I decided it was hopeless. There was nothing I, or anyone else, could do to bring her back from the brink of ruin and death. I didn't see her for several months, and didn't allow myself to think too much about her because I felt so badly about her situation.

You can imagine how shocked I was when I ran into her on campus one day, and she looked completely well and healthy. Light sparkled in her eyes. When she saw me, the happy grin on her face got even bigger. Everything about her was different.

"I've been born again!"

Before I could think better of it, I blurted out, "What in the world happened to you?" I suppose it was rude, but

I really couldn't help myself. She had come back from the walking dead.

"I've been born again!"

"You've been what?"

"Born again," she laughed. "I've made Jesus Christ the Lord of my life."

She could tell from the puzzled look on my face that I wasn't getting the connection, so she proceeded to tell me, with great enthusiasm, that she had turned to Jesus, and that He had set her free from her addiction. The desire had just gone away. One instant, she was a hopeless addict. The next, the craving had vanished.

I couldn't deny the evidence standing right in front of me, but I didn't want to accept what she was telling me. My thinking was, "If it worked for you, fine, but I've got other plans for my life." I just wanted to get away from her, and it took me at least 10 minutes to do so.

Even then, I couldn't really get away. For the next week or so, she called me every day, asking questions like, "Do you know why you're here on earth?" and "Where would you go if you died right now?"

At first, I politely tried to brush her off. But her questions haunted me. Why *was* I here? Where *would* I go if I died? Her words had impact because there was no denying that something amazing and real had happened to her. She was not the same person I'd known before.

No place for a Jewish boy

Finally, I agreed to go with her to a Bible Study.

From the moment I walked into that room full of smiling young people with open Bibles on their laps, I wanted to turn around and run. This was no place for a good Jewish boy to be! But I didn't run. Instead, I managed somehow to survive all the way to the end of a 90-minute study, hoping all the time that nobody noticed how strange and out of place I felt.

I breathed a deep sigh of relief when we finally came to the end of the evening. I didn't know that God wasn't through with me yet.

As some members of the group were saying their good-byes and making their way out into the cold Buffalo evening, the teacher sat down beside me and said he needed to talk to me.

Before I could react, he put a Bible on my lap and began leading me through the Scriptures. He showed me in Romans 3:23 and 6:23, that *all have sinned* and *the wages of sin is death*.

I immediately knew that God was speaking to me. I didn't hear any voice or have a vision of God, yet I knew He was in the room. I felt the weight of my sin and my separation from Him.

The teacher wanted me to pray with him, but even though I knew something extremely important was happening, I resisted. I enjoyed living the life of a single, carefree college student and didn't want to give it up for any reason.

My mind was reeling. I didn't want to stay and pray the prayer of salvation. I wanted to bolt out the door, run all the way home, and never come back.

Finally, I decided that whether or not I meant it, I'd better say the prayer, just to get this guy off my back.

So that's what I did.

Even as I confessed that I was a sinner and asked Jesus to take charge of my life, I wasn't sure I really meant what I was saying.

When it was finally over, I went home and tried to forget the whole thing. But something strange had happened. Over the next few days, I discovered that I had a tremendous hunger for the Bible. I just couldn't get enough of it.

I don't know what I expected to find in the New Testament. I had always thought of it as *the Christians' book*, and didn't think there would be any connection at all to what I'd learned at synagogue as a child. Imagine my shock when I dove into the Book, and immediately found references to Abraham, Moses, David and the other Jewish heroes I had heard about all my life. It was clear that *Jesus* was not the *God of the Gentiles*, as I had always been told, but was in fact *Yeshua* (Jesus' Hebrew name), the Messiah of Israel.

I nearly laughed out loud with joy as I learned that Yeshua was born to a Jewish mother in the Jewish homeland of Israel, and that all of His first followers were Jews.

I began to search through the Hebrew Scriptures and discovered that Yeshua was, in fact, the fulfillment of literally hundreds of Messianic prophecies. What a wonderful, life-changing experience this was.

Life takes a new direction

As I drew closer to God, and our Messiah, Yeshua, my goal of becoming a millionaire by the time I was 30 suddenly seemed shallow, and even a bit silly. The treasures of this world were trivial when illuminated by the great light of God's eternal love.

Over the next few weeks, as I continued to study His Word, I began to sense that God had a calling on my life. It was clear to me that He wanted me to reach my fellow Jews with the Good News of eternal life through faith in Yeshua.

Since then, that's exactly what I have endeavored to do. During that time, my relationship with Yeshua has grown stronger and deeper. I have never doubted Him, and He has walked beside me every step of the way.

Back at the University of Buffalo, I switched my major from business to theology. In 1984, after graduating with a degree in Jewish Studies and Early Jewish Christianity, I founded Congregation Shema Yisrael, a Messianic Jewish Congregation in Rochester, New York.

Our small congregation was aided by a pastor of an Assembly of God church, who graciously opened up their facility to us and gave me office space. In return, I helped out as an associate pastor.

One Sunday he invited one of the End Times preachers who was making the rounds at that time to speak. As I sat on the platform behind him, I couldn't believe what I was hearing. I struggled to control my composure as he reported that the Third Temple had been rebuilt in Jerusalem, that the red heifer had been born, and that the sacrificial system was about to be reinstated.

Because I had already spent some time living in Israel while taking part in an archaeological excavation, I knew this wasn't true. As soon as the service was over, I confronted him.

"The things you said today just aren't true."

"Well, I have pictures."

I asked him to show me, but he refused.

When I continued to press him, and involved the senior pastor in our discussion, he relented.

He opened up his briefcase and pulled out some photos that he said were of the rebuilt Temple. I recognized that the photographs were of a conservative synagogue, constructed far away from the Temple Mount.

Why do I tell you this story? Because it is an example of distortions and exaggerations that have been perpetrated upon God's people.

Jesus told us to live in constant expectation of His return. This is a good thing. But He also said,

> "So if anyone tells you, *There he is, out in the desert*, do not go out; or, *Here he is, in the in-*

ner rooms, do not believe it. For as lightning that comes from the east is visible even in the west, so will be the coming of the Son of Man." (Matthew 24:26-27)

Don't throw out the baby. . .

For many years, believers have seen almost anything that happens on the international stage as a sure sign that the Second Coming is imminent. During the first Gulf War, some hinted that Saddam Hussein fit the profile of the antichrist. Prior to World War II, Adolph Hitler and Benito Mussolini were considered prime suspects. So was Josef Stalin. When Napoleon's armies swept through Europe, many were sure that he was satan's chosen one.

There have also been many obviously erroneous predictions about the date of the world's end:

- Bernard of Thuringia calculated that the end would come in 992.
- Pope Innocent III expected the Second Coming to take place in 1284, 666 years after the rise of Islam.
- Mathematician Michael Stifel calculated that the Day of Judgment would begin at 8 a.m. on October 19, 1533.
- John Napier, the mathematician who discovered logarithms, predicted that the world would end in 1688.
- Puritan Cotton Mather chose 1697 as the year of Jesus' Second Coming.

- William Miller found a huge audience for his prediction that Jesus would return on October 22, 1844. When it didn't happen, that day became known as *The Great Disappointment.*

And the list goes on.

And what did our Lord have to say about all of this?

> "No one knows about that day or hour, not even the angels in heaven, nor the Son, but only the Father." (Matthew 24:36)

But He also said,

> "Therefore keep watch, because you do not know on what day your Lord will come." (Matthew 24:42)

Erroneous predictions have caused many to become disillusioned and *throw out the baby with the bath water.* In other words, they've stopped looking for any signs of the Messiah's return.

And yet, He is coming. Very soon. In the pages ahead, I'll tell you how I know.

Chapter Two

WHY SATAN HATES THE JEWS

Reason #1 we can know the Last Days are near:
satan is increasing his attacks on the Jews

It's a beautiful, peaceful day in Phoenix, Arizona.

Outside my office, the sky is a deep, clear blue. A couple of fluffy-looking white clouds float past overhead, pushed along by a gentle desert breeze.

It's an almost perfect day, the sort that makes you feel good just to be alive.

As I look out my window, it is difficult to believe that a vicious, bloody war is raging out there.

But it is.

Although I can't see it with my physical eyes, satan and his army of demonic angels are fighting for survival against the armies of God. Satan knows his time is running out. He is backed into a corner and striking out in any and every way he can.

Spiritual warfare rages all around us. Whether we like it or not, whether we admit it or not, we are all caught up in the midst of the battle. The Bible warns us about this:

> For our struggle is not against flesh and blood, but against the rulers, against the authorities, against the powers of this dark world and against the spiritual forces of evil in the heavenly realm. (Ephesians 6:12)

As I mentioned, satan is doing anything and everything he can to survive. One of his most important strategies involves the annihilation of the Jewish People.

Why? Because it was through the Jewish People that the Messiah came. And because the Jewish People play such an integral part in the Messiah's return, satan desperately continues to focus on their destruction in hopes of preventing the Second Coming of Yeshua.

The world vs. the Jews

Look around you and you will see that blind, unreasoning hatred of the Jewish People did not die with Adolph Hitler. The following is just a small sampling of what some *world leaders* have said about the Jewish People:

> There will be a war of extermination and a momentous massacre which will be spoken of

like the Mongolian massacres and the Crusades. No Jew will be left alive.
— *Gamal Abdel Nasser, President of Egypt* [1]

The Jew in Palestine must be exterminated.
There can be no option for those of us who
revere the name of Allah. There will only be
jihad. — *King Farouk of Egypt* [2]

There can be no compromise until every Jew
is dead and gone. — *King Idris of Libya* [3]

The entire Jewish population must be destroyed or be driven into the sea. Allah has
bestowed upon us the rare privilege of finishing what Hitler only began. Let the jihad
begin. Murder the Jews. Murder them all.
— *Haj Amin el Husseini, Grand Muslim Mufti* [4]

I realize that these quotes are a bit *dated*. But have things
really changed? Absolutely not.

Mahmoud Ahmadinejad, President of Iran, is adamant:
"Israel must be wiped off the map." [5]

Dr. Yussuf Al-Sharafi, a leader in Hamas, claims, "Israel is based only on blood and murder in order to exist,
and it will disappear, with Allah's will, through blood and
Shahids [martyrs]." [6]

And Osama Bin Laden told Al-Jazeera television, "I tell Muslims to believe in the victory of God and in Jihad against the infidels of the world. The killing of Jews and Americans is one of the greatest duties." [7]

Anti-Semitism on the Rise

In 2008, dozens of incidents like the following were reported:

- **In Poland,** a poster inviting people to a *patriotic* rally at a Catholic church proclaimed, "The kikes will not continue to split us."
- **In Germany,** a group of four men unleashed a vicious dog on five teenagers on their way home from a Jewish high school in central Berlin.
- **In the Ukraine,** a Rabbi was severely beaten by four men shouting anti-Semitic slurs.
- **In Switzerland,** an elderly Jewish man was stabbed by a stranger shouting, *"Jew!"* before the attack.
- **In France,** three policemen were suspended from a local police force after making Nazi salutes and shouting anti-Semitic insults.
- **In Ireland,** anti-Semitic slogans were painted on the home of a Jewish couple in the town of Galway. The entrance to the couple's home was vandalized with the words, *Go Home, Jew,* and a swastika was spray-painted on the driveway wall. Swastikas were also spray-painted on the windows of the house.

The list goes on and on, and no country is exempt, including the United States. Although figures are not yet in for 2008, the Jewish Anti-Defamation League reports there were 1,350 anti-Semitic incidents in the United States in 2007.

All over the world, graveyards have been desecrated. Holocaust Memorials destroyed. Houses painted with swastikas and *Jews, Go Home*. And, of course, Iranian President Mahmoud Ahmadinejad vowed that the countdown to the utter destruction of Israel has begun.

The Jewish Defense League has published a report stating that anti-Semitism is at its highest level since World War II. Much of it has been repackaged as *anti-Zionism*, or disguised as support for the Palestinian people.

I took my mother to England for her 70th birthday, and we stayed at a very nice Hilton hotel. Across the street, a group of people was handing out anti-Israel literature.

I always like to know what the opposition is up to, so I took one of their brochures. It began with a rather common and reasonable-sounding anti-Zionist argument. But on the back was much malicious nonsense lifted right out of the shameful *Protocols of the Elders of Zion*. I confronted them about it, and asked why they were spreading lies about the Jews.

Of course, I already knew the answer. Satan has hated the Children of Israel for thousands of years and has used hundreds of different men and women to attack them. And every time God is about to bring deliverance into the world, there is a concentrated effort to destroy the Jewish People.

Jewish Voice Ministries International has not been exempt. Recently, when I was in Ethiopia with one of our medical teams, we received a series of very specific e-mail threats. Whoever sent them knew I was in Ethiopia, and threatened to kill me there. In fact, the writer said our entire group was in danger and also mentioned the editor of our magazine by name.

The threats were very sophisticated. They brought swarms of FBI, Homeland Security, and ATF agents to our office in Phoenix. All of our computer hard drives were taken and the agents told us we should take the threat very seriously. They laid out a plan for protecting our property that cost us about $100,000 in landscaping plus other expenses. Of course, I felt compelled to do whatever I could to protect the members of our staff.

Satan's attempts to destroy the Jews

The first example of a satanic attempt to destroy the Jews is found in the second book of the Bible, Exodus. Some 430 years after Joseph's brothers sold him into slavery in Egypt, the Lord was about to raise up a deliverer to bring his descendants back to the Promised Land.

That hero was, of course, Moses.

Satan was determined to keep the Hebrews in slavery, so he put it into Pharaoh's heart to destroy every baby boy in Egypt.

Then Pharaoh gave this order to all his people. Every boy that is born you must throw into the Nile, but let every girl live. (Exodus 1:22)

You know the rest of the story.

Because his mother hid him from Pharaoh's killers, Moses survived and led the Children of Israel out of Egypt.

About 900 years later, satan again tried to destroy the Jewish People… this time through an evil man named Haman. God thwarted his plan through a beautiful, young queen named Esther.

Flash forward another 500 years to the birth of Jesus, sent into the world to deliver humankind from slavery to sin and death. When King Herod hears from the Magi that a future king of Israel has been born, he's not the least bit happy about it. He doesn't care at all what happens to the nations. He has a cushy deal with the Romans, and he aims to keep it that way. His rival for the throne must be eliminated.

Herod's advisers know enough about Bible prophecy to tell him that the Messiah is to be born in Bethlehem.

That settles it then. The Book of Matthew tells us that Herod gave orders to kill all the boys in Bethlehem and its vicinity who were two years old and younger. The Bible doesn't tell us how many innocent babies were murdered, how many mothers' hearts were shattered by his unspeakable cruelty. But we do know that Yeshua was not among them.

By the time Herod's soldiers reached the sleepy town of Bethlehem, Jesus, Mary and Joseph were well on their way to Egypt, having been warned by an angel to flee.

Having failed to kill the Messiah as an infant, satan changed his strategy. Not realizing that it had been God's plan all along that His Son would die for our sins, he convinced the Jewish and Roman leaders to sentence Yeshua to death.

Can't you just picture him laughing as he watched the Son of God dying on that tree? What evil delight he must have felt when Yeshua cried out, *"My God, My God, why have you forsaken me?"* (Matthew 27:46) But our Lord was quoting Scripture and, once again, satan's attempt to defeat God's purposes actually resulted in carrying them forward.

A history of persecution

We've talked about some of the many times satan has tried to stop God's plan to bring a deliverer into the world through the Jews. He has failed miserably every time. But he won't give up.

In the centuries after Yeshua's crucifixion and resurrection, the Jewish People have often been subjected to vicious attacks, both as individuals and as a people group.

As many as one million Jews died when the Roman army destroyed the Temple and burned the city of Jerusalem in A.D. 70. Thousands more — possibly hundreds of thousands — were massacred during the Crusades, including the entire populations of Prague and Cologne.

There has never been a time when the Jewish People have not been victimized by satan's savage attacks against them. Consider what took place during the Spanish Inquisition. In his book, *Our Hands Are Stained with Blood*, [8] my friend Dr. Michael L. Brown writes that during the Inquisition:

> There was a witch hunt against baptized Jews who maintained any vestige of Jewishness! These Catholic Jews (called 'Marranos,' 'Conversos' or 'New Christians'), violently forced to convert in the first place, were carefully watched to see if they were practicing 'heresy.' Heretical practices included failure to eat pork; failure to work on Saturday; failure to wear one's best clothes on Sunday; keeping the biblical feasts; observing any Jewish customs of any kind; saying any Jewish prayers; preparing food according to Jewish law; associating with non-baptized Jews; and intermarriage of children of Marrano families with children of other Marrano families.

Dr. Brown continues,

Violators, or frequently those merely accused of being violators, would have property confiscated. They would be subjected to harsh confinement and horrible torture, leading to mock trials, degradation and often death at the stake.

According to Brown, an estimated 30,000 Marranos were burned alive, and many more were strangled, after confessing to *heretical* behavior. "In addition to this, in 1492, all non-baptized Jews were expelled from [Spain]. Stripped of their possessions, and without any means to defend themselves, the sentence of mass expulsion against these poor souls was virtually a sentence of mass death. Those who *converted* did not fare much better — they were treated as second-class citizens by other Catholics and just one wrong move could consign them to the fire."

Here is a sampling of other horrors the Jewish People have endured:

- 1182 — Jews are expelled from France, and all their property confiscated.
- 1289 — The council of Vienna orders Jews to wear a round patch on their clothing.
- 1290 — Jews are expelled from England.
- 1294 — Jews are expelled from Bern, Switzerland.
- 1347 — Thousands of Jews are massacred after being

charged that they started the Black Death by placing poison in wells.

- 1494 — All Jews in the city of Trent, in Northern Italy, are massacred after a rumor spreads that they have murdered a Christian boy for religious purposes.
- 1497 — Jews are expelled from Portugal.
- 1826 — Pope Leo decrees that Jews are to be confined to ghettos and their property confiscated.

The list of what the Jewish People have suffered could go on for pages and fill an entire book. But despite these horrible injustices, and even though the country of Israel disappeared from the map of the world, the Jewish People maintained their identity. They maintained their identity despite threats by despots like Pharaoh, Herod, and — possibly the worst of them all, Adolph Hitler.

Now Hitler was not some ancient barbarian who was controlled by fairy tales and superstitions. He was a barbarian all right. But he was also an educated, modern man, surrounded by other educated men. Together they carried out the worst mass murder in human history.

The infamous Adolph Eichmann, who was hanged for his crimes in 1962, once said, "Throughout history men have dreamed of destroying the children of Abraham."

True. But the question remains, *why?*

Interestingly enough, at his trial prior to his execution, Eichmann showed no signs of anti-Semitism. Nor did he express any remorse for his role in sending millions of innocent men, women, and children to their deaths. He seemed to be an ordinary man. His life is a frightening example of what satan can do when he has control of a *regular fellow*.

Some people look at what the Jewish People have endured, at the unreasoning hatred directed at them, and say, "It makes no sense."

But it makes absolute sense to me.

Satan sentenced to death

It all begins in the third chapter of Genesis.

In the 15th verse of that chapter, God pronounces a curse upon satan, whose trickery has brought sin into the world:

> "And I will put enmity between you and the
> woman, and between your offspring and hers;
> he will crush your head, and you will strike
> his heel." (Genesis 3:15)

This is the Bible's very first prophecy of the Messiah's triumph over satan. Biblical scholars call this the *Proto-Evangelion*, which means *First Gospel*. In other words, thousands of years before Yeshua came to proclaim freedom to those held captive by sin, God told satan, *the day will come when your head will be crushed and it will be through the seed of the woman.*

The most important thing to note here is that ever since God pronounced this curse on him, satan has known that his days are numbered. He has already been condemned, and he has been doing everything within his power to keep that sentence from being carried out.

Satan is also very familiar with God's promise to Abraham, recorded in the 12th chapter of Genesis:

> "I will make you into a great nation
> and I will bless you;
> I will make your name great,
> and you will be a blessing.
> I will bless those who bless you, and
> whoever curses you I will curse;
> and all peoples on earth will be
> blessed through you." (Genesis 12:2-3)

God's promise that *all people on earth will be blessed through you* is a prophecy that the Messiah will come through Abraham's descendants; the One who will free mankind from bondage to sin and satan.

But God's plan was not completed with the resurrection, or with Yeshua's ascension. Read your local newspaper and you'll see immediately that this is true. Evil surrounds us on all sides — crime, war, terrorism, disease, child abuse, racism and hatred. Drive-by shootings are commonplace in every major American city. Suicide bombers kill and maim thousands of innocent people every year in Iraq, Afghanistan, and the Middle East. Diseases like cancer and AIDS kill millions of people every year.

But when the Messiah returns, evil will be vanquished, and all of these things will disappear while He reigns on earth. When Yeshua returns in judgment, all evil will be destroyed—and that is bad news indeed for our ancient enemy, the devil.

Despite the fact that satan has been outmaneuvered and outwitted by God again and again, he is no dummy. He knows the signs of the times. He sees the Jewish People returning to Israel, and the panic stirs in his black heart.

He knows that he must strike quickly and decisively. He doesn't have a chance, but he will never give up until he is completely destroyed.

Understand that satan is not God's opposite. Compared to the might and majesty of God, the devil is nothing more than a pesky mosquito. It's almost amusing to think of satan and all his demons going to war against God. It's like a band of primitive islanders armed with spears, jammed into a couple of leaky canoes, going up against the entire United States Navy.

It is absolutely no contest, but our adversary is determined to cause as much damage as he can with the few puny weapons in his arsenal — especially as he sees his time running out.

Chapter Three:

WHATEVER HAPPENED TO THE AMALEKITES? OR IS GOD FINISHED WITH THE JEWS?

Reason #2 we can know the Last Days are near:
Scattered Jews are returning to Israel in record numbers

By man's logic, Israel should not exist. She should have disappeared hundreds, or even thousands of years ago.

Read through the first few books of the Old Testament, and you'll learn about some of Israel's ancient neighbors. The Amalekites, the Hittites, the Jebusites, Canaanites and those bad old guys, the Philistines. On and on it goes.

But when was the last time you saw anything about the Amalekites on the evening news?

All of those nations have vanished. But Israel remains, even though she has been overrun by foreign oppressors many times, and her People are scattered around the world. Even before Israel was re-established as a country in 1948, these dispersed Jews retained their cultural identity. The fact that they were not absorbed completely into the cultures that took them in is one of the great evidences for God's existence and faithfulness.

> And it shall come to pass in that day, that the Lord shall set His hand again the second time to recover the remnant of His people, which shall be left, from Assyria, and from Egypt, and from Pathros, and from Cush, and from Elam, and from Shinar, and from Hamath, and from the islands of the sea. (Isaiah 11:11, KJV)

This is an incredible statement, which refers to the Children of Abraham who have been banished to Africa, Asia, and the islands of the sea — into the remotest corners of the earth. The Bible calls them the *Outcasts of Israel*.

I have gone to some of these remote areas, meeting Jews in China, Siberia, India and other countries half-way across the globe from Israel. I'll never forget the Jewish gentleman I met in Haiphong, China who asked me if I was Jewish.

When I said that I was, he looked surprised and said, "Funny, you don't look Jewish."

God knows His People

The Ten Lost Tribes of Israel aren't really lost. God knows where they are, and He is going to bring them together, along with the dispersed of Judah, who have also been outcasts since the Temple was destroyed in A.D. 70. All of these People are wandering in a place outside of their home. They're all transient. And God is committed to bringing them home to Israel.

In countries like Ethiopia, Jewish communities have been found practicing a form of Judaism that pre-dates Rabbinic (Talmudic) Judaism.

Recently, in the isolated state of Mizoram, in northeastern India, I met with Jews who have been cut off from the rest of the world for hundreds of years. Their existence wasn't even discovered until the middle of the 19th century. There they were, hidden away, hundreds of miles away from any outside influence. Yet they retained Jewish customs and traditions.

Dreams and visions in India

There are other Jews scattered throughout this part of India, Burma and Bangladesh's Chittagong District. Until the last generation, they were animists.

In other words, they worshipped the spirits of birds, tigers, trees, waterfalls, and other aspects of God's creation. (Naturally, this reminds me of Paul's words in the first chapter of Romans regarding those who *became fools and exchanged the glory of the immortal God for images made to look like mortal man and birds and animals and reptiles.* (Romans 1:22-23)

These tribalists say that they had completely lost touch with their Jewish roots during centuries of exile in Asia.

Then, about 20 or 25 years ago, some of their leaders began having *dreams and revelations* regarding who they were as a people. They returned to the worship of one God, and although they did not have copies of the Bible to read, something of a *religious revival* swept through them, and they began to live in a way that is consistent with Judeo-Christian morality and teaching.

In an article written for the Jerusalem Center for Public Affairs, Nathan Katz and Ellen S. Goldberg wrote,

> No one knows quite what to make of these tribals... nor what to do about their claims to Jewish identity and their aspiration to immigrate to Israel. Several groups, especially Jerusalem-based Amishav, have made efforts to reintroduce them to Jewish observance and some have undergone Orthodox conversion. The Israeli ambassador to Burma, Itiel Pann, is sympathetic to their cause, but the Israel government recently denied visitor visas to a delegation of Indian tribals. [9]

The Israeli government may not know what to make of these people, but I do.

God is calling His People home to Israel — even those who at one time had no interest!

Isaiah's Prophecy is being fulfilled

Clearly, Isaiah — and other prophets of God — fore-saw a time when the Jewish People would be gathered from the nations where they had been scattered and return to the Promised Land. Today, this prophecy is being fulfilled at an incredible rate.

> **This *aliyah*, or return of Jews to their biblical homeland, is yet another important sign that the Messiah's coming is approaching.**

I put together my first tour of Israel back in January of 1984. There was a group of 15 or so who traveled the land on a mini-bus. If I remember correctly, we were in the Golan Heights when a woman asked our tour guide, "Why is it called the State of Israel, and not the Nation of Israel?"

Without even pausing to think about her question, our guide answered, "Because the Nation of Israel is scattered throughout the world. And only when the People of Israel come back to the Land will we call the State of Israel the Nation of Israel."

There is an important distinction to be made between the geographical landmass that bears the name of Israel, and the People scattered all around the world who make up the

Nation of Israel. The point could be made that Israel is the only Nation of this sort in history.

Is God finished with the Jews?

If you grew up in a Christian home, you may have been taught that God is finished with the Jews.

This is absolutely not true!

God has preserved the Jewish People not only because of His love for them, but because Israel plays a vital role in the return of His Son.

There are literally dozens of Bible passages that show the important role of the Jewish People in the Last Days of planet earth. Listen to the words of Yeshua Himself:

> "O Jerusalem, Jerusalem, you who kill the prophets and stone those sent to you, how often I have longed to gather your children together, as a hen gathers her chicks under her wings, but you were not willing. Look, your house is left to you desolate. For I tell you, you will not see Me again until you say, *Blessed is He who comes in the name of the Lord.*" (Matthew 23:37-39)

Clearly, Messiah was talking to the Jews who lived in the city of Jerusalem. Today, they continue to reject and deny Him. Tomorrow, they will see Him coming in power and glory as affirmed by the Prophet Zechariah:

"And I will pour out on the house of David and the inhabitants of Jerusalem a spirit of grace and supplication. They will look on me, the one they have pierced, and they will mourn for him as one mourns for an only child, and grieve bitterly for him as one grieves for a firstborn son. On that day the weeping in Jerusalem will be great, like the weeping of Hadad Rimmon in the plain of Megiddo." (Zechariah 12:10-11)

Once again, we see that Jerusalem will be filled with descendants of David when the Lord returns. This would have been impossible before Israel was re-established in 1948. And it would have been highly implausible before Jerusalem was recaptured by Israeli forces in 1967.

It's difficult to understand how so many Christians can think that God has turned His back on all of the promises He made to the Jewish People. When God says something, He means it, and He will not change His mind.

There used to be a bumper sticker that read, "God said it, I believe it, and that settles it."

I haven't seen that saying in a long time, but I still think it's a good one to live by, and it speaks to me of what the Bible says about God's relationship with the Jews.

As German evangelist Ludwig Schneider wrote, "Christians note the veil over the eyes of Jews that blinds them from seeing the Messiah, but when non-Jews don't believe that God's promises to Israel are still valid today, there is a veil over their hearts which encompasses all the nations." [10]

God always keeps His promises

In the second chapter of Judges, the Angel of the LORD tells the Children of Israel,

> "I brought you up out of Egypt and led you into the land that I swore to give to your forefathers. I said, *I will never break my covenant with you...*" (Judges 2:1)

The Book of Hebrews, written to the Jewish believers, says:

> Let us hold unswervingly to the hope we profess, for He who promised is faithful. (Hebrews 10:23)

Daniel 9:27 tells us that the Temple will be rebuilt in Jerusalem, and in 2 Thessalonians 2:4, Paul says that the antichrist will *set himself up in God's temple.*

How can any of this happen if God has rejected the Jewish People en masse? There is only one answer.

It can't.

Clearly, the Jewish People play an integral role in God's plans for this planet of ours.

Origen and Augustine

In view of these passages, and many others that affirm the role of the Jewish People in God's ultimate plan for His creation, how did so many come to believe that God is finished with the Jews?

The change did not happen quickly.

As late as the middle of the second century, Justin Martyr wrote,

> I, and all other entirely Orthodox Christians, know that there will be a resurrection of the flesh, and also a thousand years in a Jerusalem built up and adorned and enlarged, as the prophets Ezekiel and Isaiah, and all the rest, acknowledge.

He went on to say that those who did not acknowledge these truths were "godless and impious heretics..." [11]

It wasn't until the following century that Origen, a church leader from Alexandria, began to teach that all of the Bible's prophecies related to Israel were spiritual in nature, and thus not to be taken literally. According to Origen, there was no special place for the Jewish People in the fulfillment of God's plan on earth. The mantle had been passed to the Church. The Jews had become irrelevant.

The Church rejected Origen's teachings and branded him a heretic. He was excommunicated — twice. But his teaching would not go away. By the Council of Nicea in 325 it had taken root. In his book, *The Church and the Jews, The Biblical Relationship*,[12] Daniel Gruber writes:

> The anti-Israel spirit of this meeting can be seen in some of the statements of the council: 'Let us then have nothing in common with the most hostile rabble of the Jews...In pursuing this course with a unanimous consent, let us withdraw ourselves...from that most odious fellowship [the Jews]'.

Gruber adds,

> There is no doubt that this council was an important turning point in the history of the Church. Israel was cast aside and the Church officially became the 'new Israel.'

Replacement Theology became especially prominent in the fifth century, when St. Augustine wrote in *The City of God*, that the Christian Church had replaced the Jews as God's Chosen People. In fact, Augustine considered unbelieving Jews to be the enemy of God's people.

Augustine came to his conclusion despite the fact that the prophet Jeremiah says,

> 'Only if the heavens above can be measured and the foundations of the earth below be

searched out will I reject the descendants of
Israel because of all they have done,' declares
the LORD. (Jeremiah 31:37)

God acknowledges in this passage that the People of
Israel have done rebellious and sinful things. He says, in
essence, I would certainly have a right to reject the Jewish
People because of all they have done, but I won't do it. Ever.

Augustine's teaching played a major role in the devel-
opment of Replacement Theology, and opened the door to
more than 1,500 years of Jewish persecution at the hands of
so-called Christians. Of course, those who have persecuted
the Jews are not really Christians at all. But believers need
to understand that most Jews do not know the difference
between those who have a real relationship with Yeshua, and
those who merely twist His Word to justify their evil acts.

A closer look at Jeremiah 31

Before we move on to look at another reason why I
believe the Last Days are upon us, let's take a closer look
at God's promises to the Jewish People in the 31st chapter
of Jeremiah:

> "The time is coming," declares the LORD,
> "when I will make a new covenant with the
> house of Israel and with the house of Judah. It
> will not be like the covenant I made with their
> forefathers when I took them by the hand to

lead them out of Egypt, because they broke my covenant, though I was a husband to them," declares the LORD. "This is the covenant I will make with the house of Israel after that time," declares the LORD. "I will put my law in their minds and write it on their hearts. I will be their God, and they will be my people." (Jeremiah 31:31-33)

The passage goes on to say:

"...they will all know me, from the least of them to the greatest, declares the LORD. For I will forgive their wickedness and will remember their sins no more." (Jeremiah 31:34)

How can anyone read these passages with an open mind and still say that God has terminated His covenant with Israel? It simply isn't possible. God can't turn His back on His covenant, because He would then be a liar and a promise-breaker, in complete contradiction of everything we know about Him.

In Romans 11:29, Paul reiterates God's promises to Israel from Jeremiah 31: *God's gifts and His call are irrevocable.* Speaking of the Jewish People, he writes,

Just as you who were at one time disobedient to God have now received mercy as a result of their disobedience, so they too have now become disobedient in order that they too may now receive mercy as a result of God's mercy to you. For God has bound all men over to disobedience so that He may have mercy on them all. (Romans 11:30-32)

Understanding God's new covenant with His Chosen People is an important key to uncovering His plan for the Last Days. There are several important ways in which this new covenant differs from the laws that were given to Moses on Mount Sinai:

1. It is internal, not external

Whereas the covenant made with Moses was written on tablets of stone, God's new covenant is written on the hearts of those who belong to Him.

The laws of God have not been eradicated. He has written them on our hearts and minds and given us the power to live in obedience through the indwelling Holy Spirit. During His earthly ministry, Yeshua often spoke against the Jewish leaders who bound up God's People with a jumble of man-made laws that were nearly impossible to follow. (See Matthew 23:4, for example.) Over 2,000 years since then, the burden has not been lightened. But in these Last Days, we can expect to see the hearts of Jewish People grow tender toward God as He writes His laws on their hearts.

2. It is about a personal relationship

The Mosaic covenant was about obedience. The Israelites saw God's might and power, but they did not have a personal relationship with Him. In the beginning of their exodus from Egypt, the only way they could have access to God was through Moses. Later on, the priests served as intermediaries between the Jews and their God.

By contrast, the New Covenant is a living, breathing relationship with God. It is all about knowing Him personally, and not just knowing about Him.

3. It is all about intimacy

When I was a boy, I spent a lot of time learning *about* God. I heard all of the amazing stories about the miracles He had performed through the heroes of the Bible. I learned how He parted the Red Sea, gave the Children of Israel manna in the wilderness, saved Daniel from the Lion's Den and so on.

But it wasn't much different from what I learned in school *about* George Washington and Abraham Lincoln. I knew that George Washington was the first President of the United States, and that he was often referred to as *The Father of Our Country*. I knew that Abraham Lincoln had freed the slaves, that he had preserved the country during the Civil War, and that he had been assassinated by John Wilkes Booth. But I never felt like I *knew* Washington or Lincoln and neither did I feel like I *knew* God.

It was only when I surrendered to Yeshua that I discovered I could have an intimate friendship with the Creator of the universe. Now I don't just know *about* Him. I know Him personally. I believe, according to Jeremiah 31, that a day is coming when every Jewish man, woman and child will know Him in this way.

4. It's all about forgiveness

There was no real forgiveness of sins under the Mosaic Law. Instead, yearly sacrifices were required in order to push the debt forward for another year. You might think of it as being like a balloon payment on a mortgage. You could delay payment for a while, even for many years. But sooner or later it was going to come due. And then, watch out!

But the blood of Yeshua cancels sin forever!

What I want you to see here is that the promise of eternal forgiveness was made to the Children of Israel. Jesus Himself said that He had been sent to *"the lost sheep of Israel."* (Matthew 15:24) When a Gentile believer accepts Jesus as his Lord or Savior, he or she is grafted — or adopted — into God's family, and thus is able to partake of all the promises that were first delivered through the Prophet Jeremiah. This is why, Paul writes,

> ... some of the branches have been broken off, and you, though a wild olive shoot, have been grafted in among the others and now share in the nourishing sap from the olive root... (Romans 11:17)

Remember also that in John 15:5, Yeshua said, *"I am the vine; you are the branches..."*

Jesus was a Jew, born into a Jewish family in a Jewish Nation. He grew up following all of the Jewish rituals and customs. His disciples were all Jewish, and He spent His time on earth preaching to the Jewish People.

He is the Messiah who fulfilled the prophecies of the Jewish Scriptures. And yet, God loves the world so much that He gave His only Son for all who believe, Jewish and Gentile alike.

As a Jew, it makes me sad to see that many American Christians have very little understanding of their Jewish roots.

But it makes me feel even worse when well-meaning Christians tell me, "Brother, you're not a Jew anymore. You're a Christian."

No, I'm still a Jew. I'm a Jew who believes in Yeshua as Messiah and Son of God — but I'm still a Jew. One who joyfully lives in the daily reality of God's fulfilled promises and His love.

God's promises are another reminder that He has not discarded the Jewish People, and that Jews play a vital role in the unfolding of the Last Days.

Besides, it is clearly not true that all Jewish People have rejected the Messiah. The first-century Church was made up primarily of Jewish believers — especially the Church in Jerusalem. The Book of Hebrews was addressed to Jewish believers.

For the last 2,000 years, there has never been a time when there were no Jewish believers. August Neander, who is considered by many to be the pre-eminent historian of the Church, was one of these.

Many Gentiles don't seem to understand that it is often a very difficult decision for a Jew to *accept Christ*. It is not a matter of praying the sinner's prayer and then going on with your life. It can mean that you are disowned by your family and rejected by life-long friends. The Jewish believer will be made to feel that he or she is *joining the enemy*, due to the long history of *the Church's* persecution against the Jews.

And yet, despite the difficulties, Jews are turning to Yeshua in record numbers.

The Last Days are clearly just around the bend.

Chapter Four

SOMETHING'S HAPPENING OUT THERE

Reason #3 we can know the Last Days are near:
Many thousands of Jews are turning to Yeshua

Moscow 1995

I stood in the middle of Olympic Stadium, listening with my eyes closed as a chorus of voices lifted up songs of praise to Yeshua, our Messiah, King Jesus.

I opened my eyes and gazed around me at the near capacity crowd. The bleachers were filled with at least 15,000 people, maybe more. *At least half were Jewish.* Most of them were on their feet, signifying that they wanted to accept my invitation to surrender their lives to Yeshua.

My mind went back to the Bible's account of what happened on the Day of Pentecost, 2,000 years ago, when the Holy Spirit was given to the apostles in Jerusalem. It was only fitting that this thrilling event in Moscow should be happening during the feast of Shavuot, corresponding to the feast the New Testament calls Pentecost — the day the Holy Spirit was given to Yeshua's disciples.

Outside, Jewish *anti-missionaries,* many of whom had come all the way from the United States and Israel, were doing everything within their power to stop us.

"Jesus is not for you!" they shouted at people making their way into the stadium. "These foreigners are apostates. They have ruined themselves with Christianity, and now they are trying to destroy you with it."

Their cries made little impact. Clearly, Jews in the former Soviet Union were eager to hear about God, and His Messiah.

Our international music and dance festivals in the former Soviet Union began in small concert halls that held a few hundred people at most. Within months, these halls could not begin to contain the crowds that turned out. Soon, entire stadiums were filled with Jewish People anxious to hear what we had to say about Messiah Yeshua.

More than half a million people in all, including many thousands of Jewish People, attended those festivals. Millions more saw them on television. More than 250,000 responded to invitations to receive Yeshua as Lord and Savior, and our conservative estimates are that upwards of 40% were Jewish.

Spiritual hunger in Russia

While I was still serving as senior Rabbi for a Messianic congregation in Rochester, New York, God put it on my heart to take the Gospel to Jews in the Soviet Union. I knew the desire had come from God, because everything was going so well in my life at the time. I had every reason in the world to stay right where I was, in my hometown. Our congregation had grown from six founding members to more than 150 in just a few years. We had recently purchased our own building. I was comfortable, well-paid, and surrounded by people I loved.

Yet my heart was burning with a desire to share the Messiah with the persecuted Jews of Russia, those who were known at the time as *Refuseniks*. These were people who wanted to preserve their Jewish identity, but were forbidden to do so by the communist authorities. Some, who wanted to migrate to Israel, had their homes taken away from them, or were imprisoned in labor camps. There was no room for faith of any kind under communist rule.

I felt God's pain for these people. His heart was breaking for them, and so was mine.

In 1990, I traveled to Russia for the first time with five other Messianic believers. We planned to be there for only six days, had a list of five or six phone numbers, no *official* guide or contacts, and basically had no idea what was going to happen when we got there.

We were traveling light, because we had to make room in our luggage for 300 Bibles and 3,000 pieces of literature about the Messiah. I remember asking one of our team members, "How in the world are we going to hand out 300 Bibles in just six days?"

Yeshua had an answer to that. "Oh, ye of little faith." (Matthew 6:30, KJV)

And yet, for the first couple of days after our arrival in Moscow, it seemed my lack of faith was completely justified. Every one of the phone numbers I dialed was wrong. People had moved away and left no forwarding phone number or other information. It was one dead end after another.

That's when one of the members of our group had a revolutionary idea.

"We need to pray about this," he said.

We all got down on our knees before God and poured out our hearts.

"Lord, we know you brought us here and that your heart aches for suffering Jews here in Russia. Thank you for allowing us to share the wonderful news of eternal joy and salvation through faith in Messiah. Lord, we need your guidance. Show us where to go. Help us follow your leading. . ."

As we prayed, I felt optimism rising. God had brought us here to accomplish His purposes. All we had to do was trust Him.

When we got up from our knees, I felt led to call one of the numbers I'd tried several times before without getting an answer. At least I hadn't been connected to a recording telling me that the number had been disconnected, or reached someone who'd never heard of the person we were looking for.

I slowly dialed the number.

It rang once.

Twice.

Three times.

I sighed, and shook my head.

Suddenly, there was a click, and a man's voice came on the line.

"Slushayu vas." (The Russian equivalent of "Hello.")

I responded in English, explaining who I was, and what I wanted.

"Yes, you have the right number," he responded in perfect English.

That person turned out to be our guide and our translator for the rest of our time in Russia. And, over the next few days, I saw a hunger for the Gospel, the likes of which I had never seen before.

I remember walking out into the street in a Jewish area with a huge bag full of Russian-language Bibles. We pulled out a few and offered them to passersby. You would have thought we were handing out hundred-dollar bills. Within two minutes we were surrounded by at least 200 people, all of them clamoring for a Bible or a piece of literature. People were actually forcing others out of the way, fighting to get a copy of God's Word.

We let it be known that we were Jewish believers in Messiah, and word quickly spread. Over the next few days, people actually took time off work and traveled two or three hours by train to get to our hotel so we could tell them about Messiah. I saw more people come to the Lord during our six days in Russia than I had seen in 10 years of ministry in the United States.

It was absolutely life-changing!

Within a month after I returned to the United States, I got a call from the Messianic Jewish Alliance, telling me they had received a phone call from a Jewish believer named Volodya. He lived in Minsk, Belarus, some 700 miles away from St. Petersburg. Somehow (perhaps by God's grace), he had received one of the pieces of literature we had handed out, and was calling the telephone number printed on the back.

He explained that he was a member of a group of about 75 Jewish believers, and they needed someone to come to Minsk and teach them more about Messiah. He also told us that he needed training in evangelism because he felt God calling him to reach out to his own people with the message of salvation.

Over the next year, I made three trips to Minsk to work with this man and the other Jewish believers in his group. What a wonderful time we had together! We laughed. We sang. We set up classes for the children and taught them the songs and dances of Israel.

And we spent hours studying the Word of God, always coming back to biblical prophecies about the Messiah and God's plan for Israel. With excitement they would open their Bibles and show me where they had already underlined those passages. *God had already spoken to them.* I was just bringing confirmation.

Clearly, this was a sovereign work of the Lord.

Volodya told me, "We saw from chapters 9 to 11 in Romans that it is God's will for Jewish People to be saved, and this is possible only through Jesus. Some people, Jews and non-Jews, think Jews can be saved another way, but this is not what the Bible says. There is only one way to our Father: through His Son. This is the New Covenant in Jeremiah 31, is it not?"

He told me, "We want to worship God as Jews. In Romans 11, it says that 'all Israel will be saved.' It also says that Gentiles who are saved are grafted into Israel, so we are one in the Lord, even though we are different nationalities. Yet when the New Covenant came, the Jews stayed zealous for the law, according to Acts 21:20."

The man's knowledge was amazing. No one had taught him this. Everything he knew came from his own reading of the Scriptures.

It was a glorious feeling to know that the Holy Spirit was moving in the lives and hearts of Jewish People all over the world. And I was humbled when Volodya asked me, "Brother Jonathan, can you help us? How is it we should live as Jews who love Jesus?"

I could write volumes about the wonderful things I saw and experienced in the former Soviet Union over the next several years:

- The crowds who literally ran down the aisles when we gave an altar call, because they couldn't wait another moment to surrender their hearts to Messiah.
- The physical healings that took place as we worshiped the Lord in song and dance.

- The time we worried about whether we could fill a 5,000-seat hall — according to an article in the local newspaper — *and more than five times that many people showed up!*
- The constant surveillance by the KGB was troubling. Beginning with our first visit to Moscow, it was apparent that we were being followed by a couple of KGB operatives. On one occasion, I saw them watching us from their car as we handed out Gospel literature. In retrospect, it may have been dangerous, but I walked up to their car and motioned for the driver to roll down the window. When he did, I handed him a couple of our flyers — one for him and one for his partner. He didn't say anything. But he took them, and I trust that they bore fruit.

There was also the occasion when the authorities threatened to shut us down if we tried to share the Gospel. There was no way I was going to obey their edict, so I figured they'd just have to carry out their threat.

Nevertheless, I offered to reserve some seats for them.

They looked at me as if I'd lost my mind. Reserve some seats? Amused looks crossed their faces. Did I really think so many people would come that they'd have trouble finding seats?

"We'll manage," one of them said.

That night, there was such a huge crowd that they couldn't even get into the auditorium. Our program went on without a hitch, and hundreds prayed to receive Messiah.

Everywhere we went in Russia, the Ukraine and other former Soviet Republics, we saw an incredible hunger for God.

We stepped into a small Baptist church to talk to the pastor. While we were there, a young man came in off the street to ask some questions about Christianity. It *just so happened* he was Jewish, and we were able to share our faith in Yeshua. The pastor said to me, "He is not so unusual, brother. Jews in Russia also want to know the truth about God."

We saw 2,000 people respond to a small newspaper ad inviting them to hear a short Bible lecture.

I sat in crowded apartments with Russian families who listened intently as I told them through an interpreter how I had come to accept Yeshua not only as Messiah, but as my Lord and Savior.

God was clearly at work in the minds and hearts of those who were just coming out of the cold, dark shadow of communism.

But so was satan.

Satan shows himself

At one street performance in Moscow, passersby seemed genuinely interested in what we had to say until they discovered, because we were handing out invitations to one of our festivals, that we were Jewish. Then they turned on us.

"Jews, go home!" some shouted.

A stooped, gray-haired babushka screamed, "I hate Jews! You should all burn in hell for what you have done!"

She tore the invitation she had been given into little pieces, threw them on the sidewalk and then spit on them again and again to show her disgust.

Another frail grandmotherly type yelled, "A festival for Jews? You Jews are pigs! You are devils!"

The unreasoning hate on their faces was a horrible thing to see. It was easy to imagine the wave of anti-Semitism that had swept Adolph Hitler into power nearly 60 years before.

One member of our group, a young Gentile woman from Maryland, was punched in the jaw, backed against a wall and spat on. Another woman tried to hand a man a tract, only to have him throw it on the ground and yell, "Heil Hitler!"

Her response was a firm, "God bless you."

The enemy was not amused that we had come into his territory to share the Gospel with the Jewish People. He was furious, in fact. But he could not stop us!

The Bible tells us in the 11th chapter of Romans that the blindness will come off the eyes of the Jews when the full number of Gentiles has come into God's kingdom, and then the deliverer will come out of Zion.

This is yet another important reason why we can know that the Last Days are upon us.

All over the world, Jewish People are coming to faith in Yeshua. There is a direct connection to the salvation of Israel and the return of the Messiah.

Forty years ago, there was not a single Messianic Jewish congregation anywhere, and there were very few Jews who professed faith in Yeshua — several thousand at best. By 2008, there were more than 350 Messianic Jewish congregations all over the world, including at least 50 in Israel.

According to a nationwide survey, there are at least 1 million Jews in the United States who express some sort of faith in Yeshua. This does not mean, necessarily, that they have acknowledged Him as Lord and Savior. But it does mean that at the very least, they acknowledge Him as a divinely inspired teacher or prophet. Their hearts are being softened. My friend, Sid Roth, says that more than 100,000 Jews in the former Soviet Union have professed faith in Yeshua. [13]

For the most part, the international media has ignored this massive turning to the Messiah of Abraham's descendants. And yet, it is one of the great miracles of our time.

Millions of Jews are coming to the realization that choosing to follow Jesus is not the same as choosing to reject your Jewish heritage. It is possible to believe in Yeshua and be a Jew!

I was drawn to Russia and her former satellites because of the huge Jewish population there — the third largest in the world, behind only Israel and the United States. Estimates vary, but there are somewhere between 3 and 5 million Jews in the former Soviet Union, despite the fact that more than 350,000 of them have returned to Israel since the fall of communism.

It is remarkable to me that these people managed to hang on to their Jewish heritage through seven decades of communist rule, when every sort of religious expression was discouraged and persecuted. The only explanation that I can see is the will of God, and His promise that,

'He who scattered Israel will gather them and will watch over His flock like a shepherd.' (Jeremiah 31:10)

Life is very hard for many Jews in the former Soviet Bloc countries because of rampant anti-Semitism and extreme poverty. In many areas, there is open discrimination against people of Jewish heritage. They are passed over for promotions or good jobs. They are denied entrance to schools and training programs. They are blamed for any and every trouble that comes along — and especially for economic problems.

On my first trip to this part of the world, in the fall of 1990, I had an opportunity to visit the one synagogue in Leningrad (now St. Petersburg), an expansive city of five million residents. Built around the end of the 19th century, the large building probably had a seating capacity of 1,000 or more. Attached to the synagogue was a small Yeshiva (school for Jewish study). As we passed through, we saw a dozen or so men huddled together around a table studying the Scriptures.

It moved me to see the diligence of these Orthodox Jews. The caretaker of the Yeshiva was a small, devout Jewish man in his 70s. We offered to give him several Hebrew Bibles — but when he saw that they contained the New Testament he politely refused them.

All I could do was pray that God would open the eyes of His People.

Over the weeks, months and years, God has answered that prayer again and again and again.

Sandra Teplinksy, attorney, author and Jewish believer in Yeshua, was in Moscow during our historic festival at Olympic Stadium. She was on the streets with us when we were verbally and, in some cases, physically assaulted. In her book, *Out of the Darkness,* she tells what happened just a few nights later:

> The concert opened with joyful sounding notes of Hebraic praise. Colorfully costumed dancers worshipped the God of Israel. The audience clapped and nodded to the beat. Some even smiled — and quite expressively for a crowd of Muscovites. Soon it seemed the whole place was thawing from a frozen stupor, coming to life before my eyes!
>
> As the name of Yeshua was proclaimed and exalted, I knew something historic was hap-

pening. Centuries-old strongholds of anti-Semitism were being shattered, at least for a brief time. Ethnic hatreds and fears were melting under the warmth of Messiah's love.

I did not hear Jonathan's salvation message that evening. I was too engulfed in the moment, too caught up in the sense of God's imminent presence, too cognizant of the spiritual threshold we were crossing. Not normally prone to tears, I had turned into a veritable fountain. I had been touched by nothing less than God's joy at His Son's claiming His inheritance.

She goes on to say that when I gave the altar call that evening:

Only a sprinkling of folks in the nearly-full stadium (other than the festival workers) did not stand to their feet to pray a sinner's prayer. We were stunned, our hearts pounding, our minds reeling with amazement.

According to festival organizers, 30,000 people attended the concert over its three nights. (The organizers deliberately underestimate numbers to avoid exaggeration, since precise counts are impossible to obtain.) More than 10,000, they said, prayed to receive Yeshua. They estimated half of those to be Jewish, based on follow-up cards distributed at the concerts. In any case, such numbers of Jews coming to faith were indeed reminiscent of the book of Acts. [14]

Acts all over again

Over the last several years, Jews all over the world have continued to turn to Yeshua in record numbers. Not since the days of the Book of Acts have so many of Abraham's children opened their hearts to receive Messiah. Through the ministry of Jewish Voice alone, some 75,000 Jewish People have responded to altar calls in the past six years. That's less than a decade!

For me, there is no greater experience than standing in front of fellow Jews who are open to the Gospel — who are willing to hear me share how my life was changed. Sometimes I almost have to pinch myself because I am so overcome with emotion, and it's hard to believe it's really happening.

At other times, everything seems surreal, as if I'm outside myself in a fog. When that happens, I may not even know for sure what I've said. But when I come off the stage, people will pat me on the back and say, "That was awesome." When that happens, I know the Lord was speaking through me.

I know from what I've seen that God is opening long-blinded eyes and regenerating thousands of Jewish hearts every single day.

This is an obvious fulfillment of biblical prophecy — and a clear indication that the Last Days are upon us.

Chapter Five

THE GOSPEL TO THE NATIONS

Reason #4 we can know the Last Days are near:
The Gospel is being preached to the nations

"And this gospel of the kingdom will be preached in the whole world as a testimony to all nations, and then the end will come." (Matthew 24:14)

I was on an airplane, on my way home from the former Soviet Union, joyously reading God's Word, and praising Him for shining the light of His love into that part of the world, where so many had lived in darkness for years.

Reading the 24th chapter of Matthew, I came across the above verse. The passage was not new to me. I had read it many times before. Even so, as I read, I could feel a jolt of adrenalin shoot through me. The feeling was so strong, the hair on the back of my neck stood up.

Why had I never seen this before? As the word *nations* nearly leaped off the page, I knew that God was opening up a new understanding in me.

This is yet another important sign that the Last Days are upon us:

Modern technology is making it possible for the Gospel to be preached to people even in the remotest areas of the planet.

And yet, as God showed me on that airplane somewhere over Eastern Europe, there is more to this passage than is immediately apparent.

For most of us, the word *nations* brings to mind land masses, set apart by geo-political boundaries, established by man. Yet the word used in this passage of Scripture is actually the Greek term, *ethnos*, which means a race, a tribe, or, as we more commonly speak of them today, a people group.

Today, in almost every country of the world, there are a wide variety of people groups — including the Jews.

Jews are scattered all over the world. They live in almost every country, yet only a very small number of ministries are reaching out to them.

This is a great tragedy, not only because the Jewish People need to hear the Good News that Messiah has come, but because God put a high priority on reaching the Children of Israel with the Gospel.

The Apostle Paul, writing to Gentile believers in Rome, declares:

> I am not ashamed of the gospel, because it is the power of God for the salvation of everyone who believes: first for the Jew, then for the Gentile. (Romans 1:16)

This passage makes it apparent that God's intention is to bring the Gospel to the Jew first in every nation where they are scattered. Only then will the Messiah return.

Throughout his ministry, it was the Apostle Paul's practice to proclaim the Gospel *first* in the synagogues of every city he visited. Though called to be an apostle to the Gentiles (Romans 11:13), he took seriously the Lord's mandate to reach *the lost sheep of the house of Israel first.* (Matthew 10:6, KJV)

Consider Paul's commitment to this mandate:

> When they had passed through Amphipolis and Apollonia, they came to Thessalonica, where there was a Jewish synagogue. As his custom was, Paul went into the synagogue, and on three Sabbath days he reasoned with them from the Scriptures, explaining and proving that the Christ had to suffer and rise from the dead. (Acts 17:1-3)

Paul did the same thing in Salamis (Acts 13:5), Antioch (13:14), Iconium (14:1), Berea (17:10)... Well, you get the picture. Paul not only wrote that the Gospel was *to the Jew first*; he lived it out on his missionary journeys.

Unfortunately, over the centuries, this mandate to take the Gospel to the Jew first has been lost.

There are two reasons for this. The primary reason, as we've already discussed, is *Replacement Theology*. Replacement Theology teaches that the Church has supplanted Israel as the apple of God's eye — that all of God's promises to the Jews no longer apply to the physical descendants of Abraham, but rather to his spiritual descendants. According to this way of thinking, the Jewish race has no special place in God's plans, so there's no reason to make any special effort to reach them with the Gospel.

It breaks my heart to see how little the Church at-large spends on outreach to the Jewish People. Although I don't have any exact figures to back me up on this, it seems to me that if you look at how much is spent on reaching the Jews, versus the various people groups in Africa, South America or Asia, you can see that outreach to the Jews is a very low priority for most Christians.

It makes sense to me that even if someone believed it was no longer imperative to take the Gospel to the Jew first, he or she would still want to spend as much time and money reaching out to the Jewish People as to any other people group. But it doesn't happen.

Some say, "Oh, you can't reach Jews with the Gospel. They just won't listen."

Oh yes they will. In fact, today, as Yeshua's return draws ever nearer, they are listening as never before.

The Gospel is for all

Another reason why some are reluctant to try to reach the Jews with the Gospel is *Dual Covenant Theology*. Dual Covenant Theology takes a completely opposite view from Replacement Theology, but it is just as dangerous... *maybe even more dangerous*.

To put it as simply as possible, Dual Covenant Theology teaches that the Jewish People have a separate path to salvation through the Abrahamic or Mosaic Covenant. In other words, proponents of this theology believe that faith in Yeshua is not necessary for Jews to obtain salvation.

It teaches that Judaism and Christianity are both valid religions, each equally worthy of the other's full acceptance and respect. In other words, Christians ought not to challenge traditional Judaism's rejection of Jesus as the Messiah. This brand of theology grew out of a guilty conscience and good intentions. As the Christian world began to understand the extent of Jewish suffering during the Holocaust, some liberal scholars began to teach that the Jewish People had suffered enough. Further, because much of this suffering had been caused by the Church's efforts to force the Jewish People to accept Jesus, it was time to stop trying to convert them. Many Christians began believing that it was good will *not* to share the Gospel with Jewish People.

It sounds noble. Yet, the Bible declares that there is only one plan of salvation for *all people*.

> "Salvation is found in no one else, for there is no other name under heaven given to men by which we must be saved." (Acts 4:12)

Jesus Himself said,

> "I am the Way and the Truth and the Life. No one comes to the Father except through Me." (John 14:6)

As Bible believers, we have no choice but to accept this at face value. Either we believe God's Word or we don't. Either we believe that Yeshua died for the sins of all, or we don't. There is no in-between.

To every nation (*ethnos*) on earth, the Gospel is to be preached to the Jews first, and then to the Gentiles. That's what Paul did. That's what we do at Jewish Voice. I've spoken at numerous mission conferences that have banners with Romans 1:16, *The gospel is the power of God for the salvation of everyone who believes...* But they don't have the rest of the text, *first for the Jew, then for the Gentile.*

God is calling us to reach His Chosen People with the Good News of eternal salvation offered through faith in His Son.

The house is on fire!

What would you do if you looked out the window and saw that your neighbor's house was on fire? You'd spring into action before you'd even had time to think about it. You'd run over there, start banging on the door and yelling, "Get out! Get out! Your house is on fire!"

Or suppose you discovered that you had a serious health issue that required immediate treatment, but your doctor kept it from you, insisting that you were all right.

You'd be livid. "Why didn't you tell me about this?"

"Because I thought it might upset you."

"Upset me?"

"Yes, you know. I didn't want to hurt your feelings by making you feel that I don't think you're just as good as a healthy person."

Well, Jewish People who have not accepted Yeshua as Lord and Savior are trapped in a house that's burning down around them and they don't even know it. They are suffering from a deadly disease called *sin*, and they don't know that there is one cure and one cure alone — faith in God's Son.

The Apostle Paul speaks to this dilemma when he writes:

> How, then, can they call on the one they have not believed in? And how can they believe in the one of whom they have not heard? And how can they hear without someone preaching to them? And how can they preach unless they are sent? As it is written, "How beautiful

are the feet of those who bring good news!"
(Romans 10:114-15)

A few verses later, he re-emphasizes this truth with the familiar declaration: *so then faith comes by hearing, and hearing by the word of God.* (Romans 10:17, NKJV)

If you read this passage in context, you'll see it is talking about the restoration of the Jewish People. In our outreaches in the former Soviet Union over the last 18 years, I have seen thousands of Jewish People come forward in altar calls to receive Yeshua as their Messiah. It has been in response to the proclamation of the Gospel, just as Paul taught.

It is not loving or kind to turn away from people when their house is on fire because you don't want to get them upset. It is not kind to avoid telling people about serious issues they have because you don't want to hurt their feelings.

If you have Jewish friends, it would be far better to tell them, "I'm an evangelical Christian, and that means I'm compelled to share the Gospel with all people. That means I can't exclude you. But please know that my love for you is not dependent upon your response. My commitment to you as my friend is unconditional."

I understand that it can be difficult to rock the boat and risk offending someone, especially when you know the person won't hesitate to respond defensively. Better to offend, than let them spend a billion years in hell!

All over the world, Jewish non-believers are living in a house on fire and don't even know it. We can put out that fire with the Living Water that comes through faith in Yeshua. I believe that every time a Jewish person turns to faith in Yeshua, we move that much closer to our Lord's return.

God loves the Jewish People. He always has and He always will. He wants to see every son and daughter of Abraham living happily in His kingdom. He loves them so much He sent His only Son to die for them. But if they turn their backs on that sacrifice, there's nothing more He can do.

If you find yourself unable to talk to your Jewish friends about Yeshua — or if you don't know anyone who is Jewish, you can at least support ministries who are reaching out to the Jewish People.

After the Iron Curtain fell, I saw many ministries going into Russia, but the Jewish community was not being reached effectively. So we came in and did events for the Jewish community — and we found that Jews are absolutely reachable with the Gospel.

If you have Jewish friends, they are in your life for a reason. And if you are a lover of Israel, you are not expressing that love biblically by affirming that Jews are fine without Jesus. They're not. You need to tactfully, prayerfully, share with them in word and deed. Let the light of the Messiah's love shine through you. Talk to them with respect, tact and appreciation. The right attitude can make such a difference!

I've heard it said that a missionary is someone who travels overseas. And in Jewish ministry, we have to cross a sea of misunderstanding in order to reach a people who have been brought up to believe that Christians are the enemy.

Thankfully, many Christian leaders do understand the importance of reaching Jews with the Gospel. Fuller Theological Seminary, in Pasadena, California, issued the following statement:

> ... We wish to charge the Church, as a whole, to do more than merely include the Jewish People in their evangelistic outreach. We would encourage an active response to the mandate of Romans 1:16, calling for evangelism 'to the Jew first.' For this we have the precedent of a great Jewish missionary, the Apostle Paul. Though sent to the Gentile world, he never relinquished his burden for his own kinsmen after the flesh. Wherever he traveled, he first visited the synagogue before presenting Christ to the Gentiles. So it must be in every generation. We must provide a priority opportunity for our Jewish friends to respond to the Messiah... we feel it incumbent on Christians in all traditions to reinstate the work of Jewish evangelism in their missionary obedience. Jewish-oriented programs should be developed. Appropriate agencies for Jewish evangelism should be formed. And churches everywhere should support those existing institutions which are

faithfully and lovingly bearing a Christian witness to the Jewish People. [15]

The Lausanne Consultation on Jewish Evangelism also noted that "there is...a great responsibility laid upon the Church to share Messiah with the Jewish People," and challenged, "we do call the Church to restore ministry among this covenanted People of God to its biblical place in the strategy of World Evangelism." [16]

Encouraging words, to be sure. And just one more evidence that Messiah's return is at hand.

Chapter Six

THE MYSTERY OF THE TWO MESSIAHS

Reason #5 we can know the Last Days are near:
The stage is set for Messiah's return

You probably didn't hear about the *Messianic controversy* that took place in Israel in 2007.

Although it caused quite a stir in Israel, for some reason it didn't make much of a splash in America. It almost seemed like someone was trying to keep a lid on it. Strange, especially when you consider that our media feeds on controversy — and this one certainly should have been a ratings winner.

It started when Rabbi Yitzchak Kaduri died in Israel in February of 2006. The Rabbi was so popular that 300,000 people came to his funeral. Kaduri was a highly regarded Sephardic Rabbi, said to be more than 100 years old.

About two years before he died, Rabbi Kaduri suddenly began warning his followers that the world was facing a series of terrible disasters.

How did he know this?

He said the Messiah had told him so.

Where, when and how did this conversation take place with the Messiah? He wouldn't say. The only thing he would say was that he would reveal the Messiah's name when the time was right.

A rumor circulated that the old rabbi had written the Messiah's name on a small piece of paper, but that he had also requested that the name not be read until one year after his death.

According to the *Israel Today* newspaper, when the note was finally opened, early in 2007, it contained a sentence of six words, with the first letter of each word spelling out the Messiah's name:

Yeshua.

The rabbi had also written, "Concerning the letter abbreviation of the Messiah's name, He will lift the people and prove that his word and law are valid. This I have signed in the month of mercy."

As you would expect, there is more to the story. The rabbi's 80-year-old son charged that the note was a forgery and said it was not written in his father's handwriting.

Aviel Schneider, the reporter who broke the story about the rabbi's note for *Israel Today* said he was urged not to publish the story. Schneider said he had never received so many e-mails, calls and other messages from people around the world — both negative and positive.

In response to his family's charge that the note was a forgery, Schneider said that in preparation for his article, he had reviewed a number of the late rabbi's hand-written papers.

That's when he got another shocker.

There were *certain symbols* drawn all over the pages.

"They were crosses," the reporter said. "In the Jewish tradition, you don't use crosses. You don't even use plus signs because they might be mistaken for crosses. But there they were, painted in his own hand."

Of course, Kaduri's family denied it, saying that the mysterious symbols were "signs of the angel."

You can just imagine the debate Schneider's story touched off in the Holy Land.

Some Jews said that even if the note was authentic, the rabbi could not possibly have been talking about Jesus of Nazareth.

Some Christians were certain that the old man had some type of encounter with the risen Lord.

And still others worried that the rabbi had been fooled by the antichrist, who, they said, is now alive in Israel and ready to assume a position of leadership.

The controversy rages

In some ways there's nothing new about this. The controversy over the identity of the Messiah has been raging for over 2,000 years. It's clear that some have made up their minds that Yeshua is not the Messiah, and nothing will convince them otherwise. Even if God re-arranged the stars in the sky to spell out, *Jesus is Lord*, or *Yeshua is the Messiah*, some would still not believe it.

But it's interesting that many Jews and Christians are in agreement that the time seems to be right for the Messiah to come. Rabbi Zalman Melamed, the head of the Beit El Yeshiva and a leader among Jews living in the West Bank, reportedly said, "Next year we will all go up freely to the Temple, which will be built, with the ashes of the red heifer, without disagreement and without questions."

The Jewish People are correct to be looking for the Messiah, but they don't realize that they are looking for the return of Jesus. They reject Him because they say He did not fulfill the Bible's prophecies about the Messiah.

Many Christians, on the other hand, accept the claims of Yeshua because He did fulfill these prophecies.

What's going on here? Are there two Messiahs?

The mystery of the two Messiahs

Sometimes it would seem this is the case.

Some of the Bible's prophecies about the Messiah point toward a suffering servant, a gentle healer who will be found ministering God's love to lepers and other outcasts. There has been a tendency among Jewish scholars, especially since the Middle Ages, to completely ignore these passages.

Other prophecies tell of a warrior king taking vengeance on God's enemies.

Many Jews reject Jesus as the Messiah because they say He did not fulfill these prophecies. Nor did He usher in an age of peace where the lamb and lion lay down together, swords are beaten into plowshares and evil is destroyed forever. And clearly, such prophecies *do* exist.

So again, Messianic prophecies can be divided into two distinct categories. I'll call them Column A and Column B. Prophecies that go into column A are those that relate to Messiah Ben-Joseph, the son of Joseph, the suffering, rejected servant. These are related to the First Coming of Yeshua. The second set of prophecies relates to Messiah Ben-David, the son of David, the conquering king. These will be fulfilled when our Lord returns to the earth in power and glory.

What many Jews fail to understand is that these Scriptures refer to the same Messiah — but two different comings. The first time Yeshua came to the earth, He gave Himself as a sacrifice for sin. When He returns, He will come at the head of a mighty army, the Conquering King who will fight against and destroy evil.

Here's just a sampling of the prophecies He fulfilled the first time He came to earth.

Yeshua:

- **Was born** in Bethlehem. (Micah 5:2)
- **Was born** to a virgin. (Isaiah 7:14)
- **Was called** out of Egypt. (Hosea 11:1)
- **Was rejected** by His own. (Isaiah 53:3)
- **Is the stone** the builders rejected, which then became the capstone. (Psalm 118:22-23)
- **Is the gentle King** who entered Jerusalem riding on a donkey. (Zechariah 9:9)

- **Was betrayed** by a friend. (Psalm 41:9)
- **Was betrayed** for 30 pieces of silver. (Zechariah 11:12-13)
- **Was accused** by false witnesses. (Psalm 35:11)
- **Healed** the blind, deaf, lame and dumb. (Isaiah 35:5-6)
- **Bore our sicknesses.** (Isaiah 53:4)
- **Was spat upon**, smitten and scourged. (Isaiah 50:6; 53:5)
- **Was hated** without a cause. (Psalm 35:19)
- **Was pierced** for our transgressions and crushed for our iniquities. (Isaiah 53:5; Zechariah 12:10; Psalm 22:16)
- **Suffered** for the sins of many. (Isaiah 53:10-12)
- **Died** among criminals. (Isaiah 53:12)
- **Was thirsty** during His execution. (Psalm 69:21)
- **Had His garments divided** among those who cast lots for them. (Psalm 22:18)
- **Cried out,** "My God, my God, why have you forsaken Me?" (Psalm 22:1)
- **Was buried** with the rich. (Isaiah 53:9)
- **Was resurrected** from the dead. (Psalm 16:10-11; 49:15)

This is a long list, I know. But it's only the beginning. Our Lord fulfilled more than 300 Old Testament prophecies. He also fulfilled prophecies like this one, from the Babylonian Talmud.

According to the story, a Rabbi met the Prophet Elijah, and asked him, "When will the Messiah come?"

"Go and ask him yourself," Elijah replied.

"Where is he sitting?" the Rabbi asked.

"At the entrance [or the gates of the city]," came the reply.

"And by what sign may I recognize him?"

"He is sitting among the poor lepers..." [17]

Like most of the prophecies I've presented, this one pictures the Messiah as the suffering servant who is rejected and mistreated for the sake of His People.

There are so many other ways Yeshua fits this description.

He could have been born in a palace. Instead, he came into this world in a barn, surrounded by smelly animals.

He could have been surrounded by servants who were there to respond to every whim. Instead, He said,

"Foxes have holes and the birds of air have nests, but the Son of Man has no place to lay His head." (Luke 9:58)

He could have called down thousands of angels to fight for Him when He was arrested, but chose instead to humbly submit Himself to those who wanted to take His life. (Matthew 26:50-54)

Author Josh McDowell calculated the odds of Jesus fulfilling only eight of the Messianic prophecies as 1 out of 10^{17} (a one followed by 17 zeros).[18] To put this into perspective, it's like covering the entire state of Texas with silver dollars two feet deep, marking one of them and having a blindfolded person pick the marked one, at random, the very first time he tries.

One mathematician figured out that the odds of one man fulfilling 60 of these prophecies would be one out of ten to the 895th power.

A brief history of three false messiahs

Many other men have claimed to be the Messiah, or have been proclaimed Messiah by their followers, but all have failed miserably. One of these men was Simon ben Kosiba (more commonly known as Simon bar Kokhba), who led a revolt against Rome in the second century. (Bar Kosiba means *Son of the Star*, which his followers took to be a reference to Numbers 24:17, *A star will come out of Jacob; a scepter will rise out of Israel.*)

As one would expect, his revolt was short-lived and came to a brutal end. According to Jewish historians, many people were burned alive wrapped in Torah scrolls. Cassius Dio, writing a century later, reported that over 580,000 people were killed. It's impossible to know if that number was accurate, although archeologists have found mass graves at several locations throughout the city. The Romans also desecrated the sacred places in Jerusalem, erecting a pig, symbol of the Tenth legion, but an abomination to Jews, on the Temple mount.

Another who claimed to be Messiah was Shabbethai Tzvi. He lived in the seventeenth century and had thousands of followers at the height of his popularity. He openly proclaimed himself as Messiah, and wrote a letter which said in part:

> The first-begotten Son of God, Shabbethai Tzvi, Messiah and Redeemer of the people of Israel, to all the sons of Israel, Peace! Since ye have been deemed worthy to behold the great day and the fulfillment of God's word by the Prophets, your lament and sorrow must be changed into joy, and your fasting into merriment; for ye shall weep no more. Rejoice with song and melody, and change the day formerly spent in sadness and sorrow into a day of jubilee, because I have appeared. [19]

His followers were disillusioned when this would-be Messiah was ordered to convert to Islam or face imprisonment or death. Shabbethai chose to convert, and then wrote to his followers, "God has made me an Ishmaelite; He commanded, and it was done."

For a while, he tried to walk a tightrope between both faiths. He told the Muslims that he was only maintaining contact with Jews because he wanted to convert them, and told the Jews he was only "pretending to be a Muslim so that he might bring them to Judaism." It wasn't long before both groups grew tired of him and he vanished into history.

Finally, the most recent of the false rabbis was the late Rabbi Menachem Schneerson. Though the rabbi himself didn't claim to be the Messiah, many of his followers clearly thought this was the case (and some still do). After he died in 1994 they expected that he would rise from the dead. They're still waiting.

Why didn't they recognize Yeshua?

Why is it that so many Jews didn't recognize Jesus when He came? Because they were looking for a Messiah who would come in power at the head of a mighty army, taking vengeance against Israel's enemies.

It's not all that surprising, really, that the Jewish People at large thought Yeshua was going to lead a war of independence against Rome. Apparently, His own disciples thought this was the case.

That's why they argued over which of them would be greatest. (Luke 9:45-48)

That's why the mother of James and John came to Him and asked Him to give her sons places of authority in His kingdom. (Matthew 20:20-24)

And, it's why the last thing the disciples asked Jesus before His ascension was, *Lord, are you at this time going to restore the kingdom to Israel?* (Acts 1:6)

Many Jews are still looking for the Messiah who comes in power and might. Among the reasons they give for rejecting Jesus:

- He did not bring world peace. (Isaiah 2:1-4)
- The entire world did not acknowledge God as the one true God. (Zechariah 14:9)
- We do not live in a world in which the leopard lies down with the goat, and the calf, lion and yearling live together in peace. (Isaiah 11:6-7)
- Nor does the lion eat straw like an ox. (Isaiah 65:25)
- Jesus did not destroy Israel's enemies. (Isaiah 29:4-6 and Isaiah 42:13)

But again, all of these things will be accomplished when our Lord returns.

His Second Coming will not be anything like the first. He's already given Himself as a sacrifice for our sins. He's granted the world 2,000 years to repent and turn to Him. Now, God's patience is exhausted, and He sends His Messiah to take vengeance against His enemies.

The Book of Revelation describes it this way:

> I saw heaven standing open and there before me was a white horse, whose rider is called Faithful and True. With justice He judges and makes war. His eyes are like blazing fire, and on His head are many crowns. He has a name written on Him that no one knows but He Himself. He is dressed in a robe dipped in blood, and His name is the Word of God.

The armies of heaven were following Him, riding on white horses and dressed in fine linen, white and clean. Out of His mouth comes a sharp sword with which to strike down the nations. "He will rule them with an iron scepter." He treads the winepress of the fury of the wrath of God Almighty. (Revelation 19:11-15)

The Apostle John goes on to describe the utter destruction that will take place:

And I saw an angel standing in the sun, who cried in a loud voice to all the birds flying in midair, "Come gather together for the great supper of God, so that you may eat the flesh of kings, generals, and mighty men, of horses and their riders, and the flesh of all people, free and slave, small and great." (Revelation 19:17-18)

There are many other prophecies related to Messiah's return. They are frightening in many ways. Frightening because they relate to the raging fire of God's wrath and the destruction of His enemies.

Some teach that the Jewish People will receive salvation at the Second Coming, when they recognize Yeshua as Messiah. And yet, it is the First Coming that reveals the Lamb of God who takes away the sins of the world. It's the First Coming that demonstrates the mercy, forgiveness and access of the loving God, who makes you ready to face the returning Messiah, who is the Lion of Judah. And I don't see forgiveness and mercy in the return. I see an angry lion with sharp teeth, devouring everyone who dares to oppose Him.

For the unbeliever, it will be a fearful thing to fall into the hands of a vengeful God. The Prophet Jeremiah says,

> "How awful that day will be! None will be like it. It will be a time of trouble for Jacob, but he will be saved out of it." (Jeremiah 30:7)

In fact, the Bible seems to indicate that two-thirds of Israel will be lost before the entire (surviving) nation turns to God.

> "I will take note of you as you pass under My rod, and I will bring you into the bond of the covenant. I will purge you of those who revolt and rebel against me. Although I will bring them out of the land where they are living, yet they will not enter the land of Israel. Then you will know that I am the LORD." (Ezekiel 20:37-38)

> "In the whole land," declares the LORD, "two-thirds will be struck down and perish; yet one-third will be left in it. This third I will bring into the fire; I will refine them like

silver and test them like gold. They will call on My name and I will answer them; I will say, *They are My People*, and they will say, *The LORD is our God.*" (Zechariah 13:8-9)

I'm convinced that we are not very far away from this cataclysmic event. All around us, there are signs that the world is being made ready for Messiah's return.

The most important of these, as we've seen, is the restoration of the People of Israel to a right relationship with God.

As I study the Scriptures, I also come across many statements about the state of the world in the Last Days that certainly apply to the world we're living in right now:

> But mark this: There will be terrible times in the Last Days. People will be lovers of themselves, lovers of money, boastful, proud, abusive, disobedient to their parents, ungrateful, unholy, without love, unforgiving, slanderous, without self-control, brutal, not lovers of the good, treacherous, rash, conceited, lovers of pleasure rather than lovers of God — having a form of godliness but denying its power. (2 Timothy 3:1-5)

Sound familiar?

First of all, you must understand that in the Last Days scoffers will come, scoffing and following their own evil desires. They will say, *"Where is this 'coming' He promised? Ever since our fathers died, everything goes on as it has since the beginning of creation."* (2 Peter 3:3-4)

And, of course, there are these powerful words of Yeshua Himself:

"Then you will be handed over to be persecuted and put to death, and you will be hated by all nations because of Me...but he who stands firm to the end will be saved. And this gospel of the kingdom will be preached in the whole world as a testimony to all nations, and then the end will come." (Matthew 24:9-14)

Now, I understand that it's easy to get "hung up" on Last Days prophecy. Whether the Lord is coming back tomorrow, next year, or two hundred years from now really shouldn't make a bit of difference in the way we live.

At the same time, I believe the Lord wants His People to recognize the *signs of the times* and know when His return is at hand.

The 12th chapter of the Book of Daniel contains a vivid prophecy of the Last Days, and then says,

"Go your way, Daniel, because the words are closed up and sealed until the time of the end. Many will be purified, made spotless and refined, but the wicked will continue to be wicked. None of the wicked will understand, but those who are wise will understand." (Daniel 12:9-10)

I urge you to be wise, to understand.

Yeshua's return is at hand.

Chapter Seven

ARE "THE TIMES OF THE GENTILES" AT AN END?

Reason #6 why we can know that the Last Days are upon us:
The times of the Gentiles are being fulfilled

I love Jerusalem — for many reasons.

I love her because she's beautiful, and because, like the Phoenix, she arose from the ashes after being destroyed by the Babylonians in 586 B.C. and again by the Romans in A.D. 70.

I love her because this is the city where Messiah taught, laid down His life for the sins of mankind, and resurrected from the dead triumphing over death. It is the city that will be convulsed in sorrow when Yeshua returns to begin His millennial reign, and all her residents look on the one they have pierced. (Zechariah 12:10-11)

This is also the city of great kings like David and Solomon, the place where the prophets and other great heroes of the Bible came to the Temple to worship God.

Yet from a human perspective, Jerusalem would not rank as one of the world's most important cities. She is not New York, Paris, London or Moscow. Even during the days when biblical history was being written in Jerusalem's streets, the city was not as significant as Alexandria, Rome or Athens.

Still today, 3,000 years after the reign of King David, a majority of the world's population believes that Jerusalem is the most important city on earth.

There is only one possible reason for Jerusalem's importance and that is simply that she is important to God. And, because Jerusalem is important to God, and to His plans for the Last Days, satan has done everything within his power to keep the city out of Jewish hands.

Why else would Jerusalem be so important? Consider:

- The city has no strategic military importance.
- Jerusalem is not an important seaport (or a seaport at all, for that matter).
- The city does not sit on an important trade route.
- The surrounding countryside is not full of important natural resources (like oil).

And yet oceans of blood have been shed over this city of more than 730,000 residents.

Jerusalem's important role in the unfolding of the Last Days was made clear when Yeshua told His disciples what would happen just before His return.

"Jerusalem will be trampled on by the Gentiles until the times of the Gentiles are fulfilled." (Luke 21:24)

The meaning of this scripture has been debated for nearly 2,000 years — and still there is no concensus.

It is clear, from the context of the passage, that Jesus was describing events on earth that would lead up to His return.

I won't tell you that I know fully *all* that He means in this important scripture — and frankly, I'm skeptical of anyone who says he does. But one thing I do know for certain is physical and spiritual restoration of Israel is key to understanding this verse. All the signs of this prophetic fulfillment have begun rapidly falling into place since the re-establishment of the State of Israel.

Once the flame of faith spread beyond the borders of Israel, Christianity became a predominantly Gentile religion. For 19 centuries, the number of Jews who openly professed faith in Yeshua was extremely small. But now, all of that is changing, and changing fast.

Gary Thoma, writing in *Christianity Today*, says:

> The rapid growth of Messianic Judaism has been remarkable. In 1967, before the Jewish People regained control of Jerusalem, there was not a single Messianic Jewish congregation in the world, and only several thousand Messianic Jews worldwide. Today, over 350

Messianic Jewish congregations — 50 in Israel alone — dot the globe. There are well
over one million Jews in the United States
who express some sort of faith in Yeshua.

Sid Roth, host of the *Messianic Vision* radio
and television show, estimates that more than
100,000 Jewish People in the former Soviet
Union alone have made professions of faith. [20]

Right now, more Jews believe in Yeshua than at any other
time in history, with the possible exception of the first century. In the last nineteen years, more Jews have come to faith
in Yeshua than in any period of time in the previous 19 centuries, and I believe there is a direct connection to Yeshua's
words about *the times of the Gentiles.*

I know that many prophecy teachers say he was referring to the restoration of Israel as a State. But my own
opinion is that they are not paying enough attention to
restoration of the People of Israel. Thousands upon thousands of Jews around the world are experiencing a restoration to their biblical homeland *and* restoration to God
through faith in Messiah. A physical and spiritual restoration is taking place.

Listen to the Apostle Paul:

I do not want you to be ignorant of this mystery, brothers, so that you may not be conceit-

ed: Israel has experienced a hardening in part until the full number of Gentiles has come in. And so all Israel will be saved... (Romans 11:25-26)

Israel and Jerusalem are back in Jewish hands. The People of Israel scattered throughout the world are returning to their Land and their God.

I want to stress, again, that this is not bad news for non-Jews. It is good news for everyone! As we will see in the next chapter, the Jews' return to God will bring *life from the dead* for all believers.

Now, if you go online and do a Google search for *times of the Gentiles*, you'll find hundreds of articles on the subject. Many of them have colorful and complicated charts showing when and where the *times of the Gentiles* began, and when they will end. It's fascinating, even though there's quite a bit of disagreement.

It's easy to get distracted by all of this and take our eyes off the big picture, which is this:

- Clearly, Israel and Jerusalem are back in Israeli hands.
- More Jews than ever before are coming to saving faith in Yeshua.

The spiritual restoration of the Jewish People is at hand. The time when God's Word finds a receptive audience *only* among the Gentiles has come to an end!

A Bit of History

When Jesus gave His prophecy about *the times of the Gentiles*, one of the events He was referring to was the destruction of the Temple, which would take place nearly 40 years later.

This occurred when the Jewish People rebelled against their Roman occupiers. At first, it seemed that God was with them, and Roman soldiers were driven out of the Holy City. Then, the nightmare happened.

Roman reinforcements stormed into Jerusalem. The Temple was destroyed. The city burned. Hundreds of thousands of men, women and children were killed. The Empire did not show a single drop of mercy.

Hundreds of prisoners were crucified in and around the city.

Those who were spared were sent into exile. They were scattered throughout the Roman Empire, and then the entire world.

Jerusalem, the City of David, became a broken-down shadow of its former glory. Much of the Israeli countryside fell into desolation. Although there were always some Jews in the Middle East, it was not until 1844 that Jews began to return to Israel in any sizable numbers.

And, of course, it was not until 104 years after the first Jews returned to the Holy Land that the State of Israel was reborn.

The return of Jews to Palestine began as a trickle. By 1900, there were an estimated 21,000 Jews in what is now Israel. But at this time, extreme persecution throughout Russia and Eastern Europe sent thousands of Jewish refugees fleeing to their biblical homeland in search of a safe haven.

And then, on November 2, 1917, the British, who had taken control of all Palestine, issued the Balfour Declaration:

> His Majesty's Government views with favour the establishment in Palestine of a national home for the Jewish People, and will use their best endeavours to facilitate the achievement of this object, it being clearly understood that nothing shall be done which may prejudice the civil and religious rights of existing non-Jewish communities in Palestine, or the right and political status enjoyed by Jews in any other country. [21]

Arthur Balfour, who gave the Balfour Declaration its name, was a former prime minister who served, in 1917, as Britain's Foreign Minister. He was also a committed Christian who believed that the return of Jews to Israel was connected to the Second Coming of Messiah.

Despite his declaration's call for a *national home for the Jewish People* in Palestine, nothing official took place. Encouraged by the Balfour Declaration, a steady stream of Jews were returning to Israel while Arab residents of the region reacted with increasing alarm. In fact, the first recorded terrorist attack on an Israeli settlement occurred in 1920.

You know what happened next. Alarmed by the return of God's People to Israel, satan entered a man named Adolph Hitler, who then murdered 6 million of the world's 18 million Jews.

Even after Hitler's defeat, when the whole world had seen the full fury of satan's rage against the Jews, it seemed that the British government — which still controlled Palestine — had turned against the Jews. Pressured by Arab countries and Muslims in the Middle East, Britain passed laws limiting the immigration of Jews to Palestine to a few thousand a year. Ships full of Jewish refugees were intercepted and forced back to Cyprus. Hundreds of Jews were placed into detention camps while the British government tried to figure out what to do with them.

How ironic that some who had been liberated from Nazi death camps were now, for all intents and purposes, imprisoned by the British.

Thus began a campaign by Jewish forces in Palestine to expel the British from the region. In 1947, the British agreed to withdraw, and the young United Nations voted to partition Palestine into Jewish and Arab sections.

The new State of Israel was recognized by the United States, the Soviet Union, and Great Britain, and admitted as a voting member of the U.N.

But satan wasn't finished. Then, as now, Israel was surrounded by enemies who wanted her wiped off the map. What's more, those enemies were much bigger, with huge armies and vastly superior firepower. Israel was outnumbered about as badly as General Custer at Little Big Horn. It seemed certain that Israel's re-establishment as a Nation was going to be short-lived. Let me rephrase that. It seemed certain to anyone who did not understand that the Children of Israel are the apple of God's eye.

The day after Israel declared herself an independent State, she was attacked by a coalition of her Arab neighbors, including Egypt, Jordan, Lebanon, Syria and Iraq. Although outnumbered by a margin of 20 to 1, the Israelis prevailed.

A couple of things happened at this time that most people don't know:

First, it was the Arab nations, and not Israel, who refused to accept the partitioning of Palestine. Had they agreed to live in peace with their new neighbor, there would be a Palestinian state in the Middle East to this very day.

Secondly, the new Israeli government offered full citizenship to the Palestinian people within her borders. It has often been implied that Israel confiscated Arab lands and homes and drove people out of the country. Yes, there was war in the region and, as with all wars, atrocities were undoubtedly committed by both sides. But it was the Muslim countries who encouraged the Palestinian people to leave Israel, and then refused to take them in, leaving them struggling for survival in squalid refugee camps.

Why am I telling you all of this? Because short of God's providence, there is no way Israel should exist. Satan has opposed her at every turn. She has felt the full force of his hatred again and again and again.

During the Cold War, the Soviet Union poured billions of dollars in weapons into the hands of Israel's enemies. The Soviets encouraged the Arab nations to attack their tiny neighbor not once, but four times, and each time God gave His People the victory!

You see, He had declared that the time of Gentile control of the Middle East had come to an end, and there was nothing anyone, including satan and all of his demons, could do about it!

The Suez War of 1956

In the early 1950s, Egypt closed the Suez Canal to Israeli ships. The United Nations ordered the canal open, but Egypt refused. Then, Egypt's President Nasser sent scores of terrorists into Israel, saying,

> Egypt has decided to dispatch her heroes, the disciples of Pharaoh and the sons of Islam and they will cleanse the land of Palestine... There will be no peace on Israel's border because we demand vengeance, and vengeance is Israel's death. [22]

His foreign minister, Muhammad Salah al-Din, added, "We shall not be satisfied except by the final obliteration of Israel from the map of the Middle East." [23]

After hundreds of Israelis were killed, Israel had no choice but to retaliate. The Egyptian army was quickly and easily defeated, and Israeli troops pushed deep into Egyptian territory before a ceasefire was declared. President Eisenhower pressured the Israeli government to return the land that had been seized and Israel complied.

The Six-Day War of 1967

On May 20, 1967 Syria's Defense Minister Hafez Assad announced,

> Our forces are now entirely ready to…explode the Zionist presence in the Arab homeland. The Syrian army, with its finger on the trigger, is united…I, as a military man, believe that the time has come to enter into a battle of annihilation. [24]

Ten days later, Israel's old enemy, President Nasser of Egypt, said,

> The armies of Egypt, Jordan, Syria and Lebanon are poised on the borders of Israel… while standing behind us are the armies of Iraq, Algeria, Kuwait, Sudan and the whole Arab nation. This act will astound the world. Today they will know that the Arabs are arranged for battle, the critical hour has arrived. We have reached the stage of serious action and not declarations. [25]

The world was astounded all right. After six days of war, the Arab coalition was utterly defeated.

The Yom Kippur War of 1973

The next war began on October 6, 1973. It was Yom Kippur, the holiest day in the Jewish calendar. Israel was not prepared for the coordinated surprise attack undertaken by Egypt and Syria. On the Golan Heights, less than 200 Israeli tanks faced an invasion of 1,400 tanks from Syria. Along the Suez Canal, some 436 Israeli soldiers were tasked with holding off an estimated 80,000 Egyptian troops.

At least nine Arab countries were actively engaged in the assault on Israel, contributing troops, weapons and/or money. Libya's Muammar al-Gaddafi sent $1 billion in military aid to Egypt.

According to jewishvirtuallibrary.org,

> Thrown onto the defensive during the first two days of fighting, Israel mobilized its reserves and eventually repulsed the invaders and carried the war deep into Syria and Egypt. The Arab states were swiftly re-supplied by sea and air from the Soviet Union, which rejected U.S. efforts to work toward an immediate ceasefire. As a result, the United States belatedly began its own airlift to Israel. Two weeks later, Egypt was saved from a disastrous defeat by the U.N.

Security Council, which had failed to act while the tide was in the Arabs' favor."

This has been life for the People of Israel. They are either at war, or being threatened by war. Today, Iran's President Mahmoud Ahmadinejad makes the same sort of threats that were once issued by Egypt's President Nasser. Hezbollah forces in Lebanon have pledged themselves to Israel's destruction, and occasionally launch rocket attacks against Israeli cities. And Israeli citizens are constantly at risk from terrorist attacks planned by Hamas, the terrorist organization that has now become the leading political party in the Palestinian regions of the Middle East. (Incidentally, Hamas' charter calls for the destruction of Israel, and its replacement with an Islamic state.)

Again, there is no way, other than God's blessing, that the Israeli People could have withstood the constant attacks against them. Not once, but at least four times, Israel has been like the little shepherd boy, David, going up against mighty Goliath. But today, just as in ancient times, God's power has defeated the giant.

I want to make it clear that I am not trying to paint the Arab or Muslim people as evil or *the enemy* in any way. Every Arab politician, every Arab soldier, every Arab civilian is someone for whom Yeshua died. God loves the Arab people every bit as much as He loves the Jews.

But His plans will be carried out through the Jews, and there is nothing any man, nation, or group of nations can do to keep that from happening.

But just as satan tried in ancient times to destroy the Jews and thwart God's plans — through people like Pharaoh, Haman and Herod — in more recent years, he has used people like Hitler, Nasser and Ahmadinejad to carry out his plans.

Sadly, the days of terror and violence are not yet over for the Jewish People. Satan is finished, but he doesn't know it. However, he won't go down without a fight.

Have you ever watched one of those cop reality shows on TV? If so, you've surely seen what happens when a suspect in a crime refuses to give up. He punches, kicks and twists as first one policeman and then another, and another, joins in the attempt to bring him down. In less than a minute, the suspect is face-first on the sidewalk, with his arms shackled behind his back and his legs pinned to the ground.

That's how I think of satan. He's cursing and biting and doing everything he can to cause trouble, but God has an unlimited supply of big, strong policeman. Soon, satan will be going down for good. And from then on, life on this planet will be nothing short of glorious.

A word about Armageddon

Before moving on to the next part of this book, I want to answer a question that always comes up whenever there is any strife in the Middle East. That question:

Is this the beginning of Armageddon?

My answer, based on my study of Scripture, is that there

are several important hallmarks of earth's final battle:

1. Nuclear weapons may be used

I believe this is what the Book of Revelation teaches. As of the writing of this book, Iran may be much closer to nuclear capability than has been communicated in the press, according to information I've been able to obtain from inside sources. The delay is in perfecting an accurate delivery system with significant range. If they come too close to achieving that, Israel will be forced to deal with Iran alone as she is the primary target. If that happens, the world will likely blame Israel for initiating the first strike.

2. Russia will be involved

Again, my study of Scripture tells me that Russia must be involved in the future invasion of Israel. And although some would strongly disagree with me, I do not think Russia is anywhere near ready for such a conflict. First, following the breakup of the Soviet Union, Russia is not the military powerhouse it once was. Second, Russia is in very poor shape economically. This is not the time to engage in military adventurism. Thirdly, the United States is still standing behind Israel, and Russia is not ready to risk an all-out confrontation with the United States.

3. The United States will turn against Israel

If I understand prophecy correctly, the day is coming when *all* the nations of the world will turn against Israel, including the United States. I fear the day that America turns her back on Israel, because that will be the beginning of the end for our beloved country. But as long as the evangelical community that loves Israel keeps praying and speaking out as *watchmen on the walls*, then American support for Israel will continue.

My prayer is that every believer will wake up, shake off our complacency, and realize the time is short. We need to be about our Father's business and do His work... *as long as it is day... Night is coming when no one can work.* (John 9:4)

Part Two

YOUR ROLE IN USHERING IN GOD'S KINGDOM

Chapter Eight

BRINGING "LIFE FROM THE DEAD"

Sammy Hellman has been my tour guide in Israel for more than 25 years.

During that time, he's become a very good friend of mine. I don't know if he's a believer. That's just not something he's open about. But he is open to Messianic thought.

He's a passionate guy who came to Israel from Romania, joined the army and has served in two wars. He loves to attend our worship services, but he always seems more like an observer than a participant.

A few years ago, something happened to Sammy that made a tremendous impression on him. I know because I've heard him tell the story several times. And yet, he still says he doesn't know what to make of it.

It happened when he was serving as a tour guide for a black Pentecostal group from the United States, and went to pick up the group at their hotel in Jerusalem.

"Out of the corner of my eye, I saw this elderly, gray-haired woman stumble on the top step."

Before anyone could help her, she tumbled all the way down a flight of 10 to 12 concrete steps. She landed hard at the bottom and lay there, motionless.

"It was a terrible fall," Sammy says. "I knew she was badly injured."

He ran to her side, picked up her arm and felt for a pulse. Nothing.

"She was dead," he says. "Beyond any shadow of a doubt."

The woman's pastor was the next to reach her.

The man bent down, began gently stroking the dead woman's hair, and quietly asked the Lord to heal her.

Then he spoke to her, "Get up, Mrs. Wilson."

Her arm twitched.

Then she began to stir.

Within a few minutes, she was sitting up and asking for someone to bring her purse, which she'd dropped during her fall.

She insisted that she didn't need a doctor. She was fine. She boarded the bus and spent the day touring Israel as planned.

Tears well up in Sammy's eyes when he remembers what he saw that day. "She was dead," he whispers. "There was no doubt about it."

He shakes his head in wonder.

"Well, Sammy, what do you think happened?" I asked.

"I don't know."

"What does this say to you?"

"I just don't know what to think about it."

Like so many Jews I know, Sammy does not want to answer the question posed by Yeshua, "Whom do you say that I am?"

In the third chapter of Acts, Peter calls upon the People of Israel to:

> Repent, then, and turn to God, so that your sins may be wiped out, that times of refreshing may come from the Lord, and that He may send the Christ, who has been appointed for you — even Jesus. He must remain in heaven until the time comes for God to restore everything... (Acts 3:19-21)

It's clear to me that this passage of Scripture is related to what Paul says in Romans 11,

> Inasmuch as I am the apostle to the Gentiles, I make much of my ministry in the hope that I may somehow arouse my own people to envy and save some of them. For if their rejection [of Jesus] is the reconciliation of the world, what will their acceptance be but life from the dead? (Romans 11:13-15)

In other words, when the Jewish People rejected God's salvation, the doors to His Kingdom were opened wide to every nation on earth.

If this happened when they rejected Messiah, just imagine how much more wonderful it's going to be when they accept Him! It's clear, in fact, that their acceptance is an important key in bringing about His return.

Israel and Japan

I spent a number of years traveling and lecturing in Japan. Why Japan? Because I was intrigued that even though only one percent of the Japanese profess faith in Jesus, most of them are members of the intelligentsia. They are doctors. They are professors and lawyers. And they have become fascinated with Israel.

They understand that the destiny of Japan is connected inseparably to the destiny of Israel. These people pray daily for the salvation of Israel, and they know that when it comes, it will directly affect their nation. It will bring *life from the dead* and *times of refreshing.*

> **The fact is, the destiny of all nations, including our own, is connected to the salvation of Israel.**

When I'm in Japan, I tell people, *If you want to see Japan saved, pray for the salvation of Israel.* When I'm in India I say, *If you want to see India saved, pray for the salvation of Israel.* Here at home in the United States, I tell people that if we want to see America turn to God in a very big way, we need to pray for the salvation of Israel.

I believe the salvation of the Jews will release the power of God and a mighty worldwide revival will result — a revival far greater than any other the world has ever seen. It will be the great outpouring spoken of by the prophet Joel:

"I will pour out my Spirit on all people. Your sons and daughters will prophesy, your old men will dream dreams, your young men will see visions. Even on my servants, both men and women, I will pour out my Spirit in those days." (Joel 2:28-29)

The very thought of this sends a frightened chill down satan's back, and he's working around the clock to try and stop it from happening. He knows that an essential part of *life from the dead* will be the crushing of his head, prophesied in Genesis 3:15.

Some scholars believe that the *life from the dead* Paul refers to in the 11th chapter of Romans is a physical resurrection of the dead that will be connected to the return of the Messiah. Most say it is talking about a spiritual renewal. But it's clear to me that this is something far greater than individual salvation.

My study of this passage has convinced me that *life from the dead* is related to the fall of Adam, and the restoration of all things. It has to do with finishing the work of atonement that restores the earth to the pre-Adamic state.

Life from the dead is the termination of the curse of man's fall from grace once and for all! It is the eradication of sin and death, our final enemies.

I certainly believe in the power of faith. I have seen miracles of healing and provision. I've seen people win a temporary reprieve from death. But I know of only two people in all of history (besides those who are living right now) who didn't eventually die. Those two: Enoch and Elijah. (Jesus did die, of course, but He came back to life!)

So a man is lying if he says he can beat death by faith. I've heard some preachers say that faith can help you beat the aging process, and it's just not so.

Don't misunderstand me. I do think there are promises in the Scriptures that we can appropriate — for health, healing, and provision. But we are still living in a world tainted by the curse pronounced on Adam and Eve.

Look around you, and you'll see evidence of that curse everywhere. A lawn or garden left to itself will soon be shaggy and overgrown with weeds. You can stand over your garden and pray that the weeds will go away, but until the curse is ended, it's probably easier to spray them with weed killer or pull them.

But I have great news! Those weeds are about to disappear. Death is about to be swallowed up in victory. We're almost to the point where we're going to wonder how in the world we ever could have been tempted to sin.

When life comes from death, we will be living in a world that operates as it was originally intended to.

A world without death

Imagine turning on the evening news or opening your morning paper and seeing nothing depressing or upsetting...

- No drive-by shootings
- No car crashes
- No suicide bombings
- No global food crisis
- No starving children in Africa
- No devastating cyclones in Southeast Asia
- No earthquakes in China

Won't it be wonderful to live in a world like that? I have good news, and even better news. The good news is that this world is on the way. The better news is that you can help speed up its arrival.

You can do that by helping the Jewish People around the world come to the saving knowledge of their Messiah and *life will come from the dead.*

A shocker from the Apostle

A couple of chapters before Paul writes about life from the dead, he makes a provocative statement.

In Romans he says,

> For I could wish that I myself were cursed
> and cut off from Christ for the sake of my
> brothers, those of my own race, the people
> of Israel. (Romans 9:3-4)

Why is this such a shocker? Because Paul is writing to Romans, not Jews.

Doesn't it seem more likely that he would be saying good things about the people of Rome? Something like, "In my estimation, Rome is the most beautiful city in the world, and you people who live there are the salt of the earth."

Once he'd said that, he'd have them on his side, and they'd listen to everything he had to say. What's the first thing any public speaker says? "It's such a pleasure to be here in _____ (insert city name here)." Appealing to civic pride almost always gets you off to a good start.

In other words, you'd expect a missionary to Japan to say, "You Japanese are the most important people in my life, and I'd give up my salvation for you." But what Paul says here is like a missionary going to the Japanese and saying, "The people of India are the great love of my life, and I would give up my salvation for them."

It's odd. And when Paul talks about giving up his salvation, he knows exactly what he's talking about, because he's experienced both the riches of Heaven and the torments of hell. And remember that he's speaking about the people who ostracized him, who stoned him, who beat him until he was unconscious and left him for dead. But despite all of this, he says he would give up, not just his life, but his eternity.

Why would he do that? There are two good reasons:

- First, Paul's statement is a revelation of God's heart for the People of Israel, and he wants the Church to share this burden with him. He is enlisting their prayer, love, and support to effect their salvation.

- Second, Paul understands the ultimate result of Israel coming to know Yeshua, which is *life from the dead* and the Messiah's return. No one can say for certain, but it seems likely to me that he might be saying, "I'd be willing to give up my salvation to see God's ultimate plan for the world accomplished."

Now is the time to hasten Yeshua's return by taking the Gospel to Jewish People all over the world.

- Believers must pray daily for the salvation of Israel.
- We must put our money into ministries that reach out to the Jewish People.

If you are involved in a church, ask what percentage of your missions budget is used for reaching the Jewish People. If it's a tiny amount, urge those in authority to reorder their priorities in light of Paul's words that the Gospel is to the Jew first, and then to the Gentiles.

Then, take a look at your own giving, and ask yourself what you could be doing, personally, to reach the lost Children of Abraham with the Good News.

Our entire planet hangs in the balance.

Someone told me a story not long ago that made me think of what happens when we pray for Israel.

A man named Mark was in the hospital dying.

Fever raged through his body. His blood pressure was dangerously low. Doctors tried everything they could think of to help him, but nothing worked. Experts were baffled by Mark's mysterious illness, and finally walked away shaking their heads.

Mark was a believer who prayed for healing, but his slide toward death continued.

Then, he woke up in the middle of the night and noticed that he now had a roommate. In the darkness of the room and the haze of his own fever, Mark couldn't discern much about the man who was now across the room in the bed near the window.

But what he could see made his heart drop. This poor fellow was in terrible shape. His arms looked as thin as pencils. His cheeks were sunken, his eyes hollow. An I.V. tube protruded from his arm.

Compassion flooded into Mark's heart.

"Lord," he prayed, "that man looks like he's really suffering. Forget about me. If it's my time to die, I'm ready. But won't you please heal that guy?"

Mark fell asleep while he was still praying.

The next thing he knew, a nurse was bringing his breakfast into his room. Sunshine streamed through the window. Mark had enjoyed his best sleep in days.

"You're looking so much better!" the nurse gasped.

"I feel better," he agreed.

"I'd better get the doctor."

When the nurse turned to leave the room, Mark saw that the bed next to the window was empty, and his heart sank.

"What happened to the other patient?" Mark called after her. "Did he die?"

She stopped suddenly, turned around and looked at him as if he'd lost his mind. "Other patient? What patient?"

"The man they put in the other bed last night. It broke my heart just to look at him."

Concern clouded her face. "There hasn't been anybody in this room but you," she said. "You must have been imagining things. You know, with your fever…"

"I wasn't hallucinating," he insisted, pointing at the other bed. "He was right there in that…"

He didn't finish the sentence as the truth hit him.

There hadn't been anyone in that bed last night. He now realized he'd been looking at the window — and seeing his own reflection.

He'd been praying for himself.

When he had been filled with compassion for someone else, and put their needs ahead of his own, God had responded and he himself had been healed.

I heard that Mark walked out of that hospital the next day, changed in body and in spirit.

You see, when you pray for the salvation of God's People, you are also praying for yourself and your family.

Their healing is your healing.

Their salvation is your salvation.

Their return to God is life from the dead for all.

Chapter Nine

RABBI, WHAT MORE CAN I DO?

People say to me, "You make it sound easy to reach Jews with the Gospel, but it's not."

Believe me, I know how resistant Jews can be.

My friend Sid Roth tells an amusing story about trying to reach his father with the Good News about Yeshua. (Sid is a Messianic Jew who wrote a wonderful book called *They Thought for Themselves*.)

It grieved Sid that his widowed father didn't want to hear anything about Yeshua, and, in fact, forbade his son to bring a New Testament into his home.

Sid thought long and hard about how to overcome his dad's resistance. Finally, inspiration hit. So he went to his father's synagogue, bought a *kosher* Jewish Publication Society Old Testament, and asked the rabbi to sign it for him.

That night, he gave the Bible to his father as a gift. Then, as they were sitting together, Sid said, "Dad, I want to read you something."

He turned to Isaiah 53 and read the entire chapter.

When he finished, the old man's face turned red and he said angrily, "I told you never to bring a New Testament into my home."

"But, Dad," Sid protested, "this is Isaiah 53 from our Scriptures." Then he showed his father that he had been reading from a kosher Bible signed by his rabbi.

Sid's dad sat there for a moment or two, looking at that rabbi's signature. Finally he spoke:

"I never trusted that rabbi."

This is how some Jewish People are. Their minds are made up, so don't confuse them with the facts.

And yet, we must understand that accepting the Lordship of Yeshua is an act that can leave a Jew cut off from his family, his friends, and his culture. It is not a decision that can be made lightly.

I was raised in synagogue life and taught that Jesus had caused the Jewish People terrible harm. You can imagine my parents' shock when I told them I had accepted Jesus. One of the first things they did was send me to the rabbi. And rather than deal with all the proofs I brought, he kept pushing the guilt button.

"Your grandfather would be rolling over in his grave if he knew you'd done this," he said. "He would do anything to stop you."

When that didn't work, he pulled out the genocide card.

"Just as Adolph Hitler tried to destroy us physically, you're aiding and abetting the enemy by seeking to destroy us spiritually."

I've heard Jewish People say, "You can't be a Jew and believe in Jesus any more than you can be a vegetarian who eats meat." It's not that they're belligerent. It's just that their worldview doesn't allow them to see how a Jew can believe in Jesus, given 2,000 years of persecution at the hands of *the Church*.

This is why it takes a special sensitivity when talking to a Jewish person about Yeshua.

I've mentioned before about all the persecution the Jewish People have undergone in the name of Jesus. During the Spanish inquisition, many Jews were deported, tortured or killed. Lands and property were confiscated, and there is some speculation that this stolen wealth was used to finance the voyage of Christopher Columbus.

In Russia, thousands of Jewish People were massacred in pogroms by *so-called Christians*. Christian peasants would put crosses on their doors so the murderers would know to leave them alone.

As a result of such atrocities, many Jews ask, "How can I accept a religion that has shed so much Jewish blood? I would be a traitor to my fathers who died if I renounced their religion and accepted Jesus."

We must get our Jewish friends and neighbors to see that the people who carried out these horrible acts were not following Yeshua. They were going against everything He taught, and they denied Him when they lifted their hands against the Jews.

Jews must come to see that they should believe in Yeshua because He is the Messiah, not because Christians are such nice people. We must show them that Yeshua is the God of whole earth, of Jews and Gentiles alike. We can show them Messianic prophecies in the Old Testament: Psalm 22, Proverbs 30:4, Isaiah 7:14, Isaiah 9:6-7, Isaiah 53, Jeremiah 31:31-34, Daniel 9:24-26, Micah 5:2 and Zechariah 12:10. We can explain that Yeshua was Jewish, as were the apostles and most of the early believers.

How do I talk to a Jew about the Gospel?

When non-Jews ask me this question, as they often do, I respond with another question:

How do you talk to anybody about the Gospel?

You have to care enough to watch, listen and see what's going on in his or her life.

For example, if you can tell that someone doesn't even believe in God, it's probably not a good idea to jump right in about Jesus being the anointed one. If someone doesn't believe in sin, you don't want to start off by talking about how Jesus bore the sins of all mankind.

Where do you start witnessing to a Jew? By praying for him. By showing through your actions that you care. By letting your light shine so they know you have a special relationship with God.

Let's turn back to Romans 11 for a second. Paul says of the Jews,

> Did they stumble so as to fall beyond recovery?
> Not at all! Rather, because of their transgression,

salvation has come to the Gentiles to make
Israel envious. (Romans 11:11)

When your Jewish friends see your close relationship
with God, they will be provoked to envy. You may not see
it. You may even feel that they find your faith amusing, in a
condescending sort of way.

But just watch what happens when trouble strikes that
Jewish friend. You'll be one of the first ones he or she will
call — and ask, "Will you please pray for me?"

Most Jewish People who come to the Lord do so at a
terminus point. They may have rejected the Gospel dozens
of times. They may have let you know in no uncertain terms
that they don't want to hear another word about your faith.
Then a tragedy happens in their life, and suddenly they're
asking questions that they've never asked before.

To sum up what I'm saying as simply as possible, it is:
Never give up. Your Jewish acquaintances may be rude to you,
and reject you. If you've always been there, showing them
love, they will turn to you when the time is right. Remember
that the Word of God never returns to Him empty. (Isaiah
55:11) It always accomplishes what God sent it to do.

In Romans 10, Paul presents the idea that it's very simple
to bring a Jew to faith in Messiah. If God can graft an un-
natural branch onto the tree, he can certainly reach the Jewish People. If you can get enough of the Word into a Jewish
person, he will come around.

Let's spend just a few minutes talking about some of the DOs and DON'Ts for talking to Jews about Yeshua, and thus hastening our Messiah's return. First the DON'Ts.

1. Don't talk about being *converted* or *being a convert to Christianity*

Anything to do with conversion is at the top of the list of negative words. To a Jew, it sounds like, "Stop being a Jew and become a Christian." We need to let Jews know that it is possible to be Jewish *and* believe in Yeshua. When you tell a Jew that he or she must "become a Christian," that person hears, "Leave the Jewish faith and become something else." And that's *not* the biblical message. That's *not* good news — and that's *not* the Gospel.

I believe it was never God's intent that Christianity would become a separate movement from Judaism. I'd love for Christians to tell their Jewish friends, "I'm not suggesting that you convert to another religion or change who you are. You were born a Jew and you'll die a Jew. But this is your Messiah, and I want you to know Him."

Honestly, Judaism is just as good as Christianity when it comes to religion. But the Bible isn't about religion, but rather, relationship. That's my message. Someone comes from a Christian background, and that's fine. Someone else comes from a Jewish background, and that's fine, too. But God is calling us to step beyond lines of background and culture so we can have a personal relationship with Him.

God loves diversity, by the way. Just look around at creation, and you'll see that this is true. There is a diversity of birds, animals, plants — and people. This is why I'm troubled that some non-Jewish people are so enamored with Judaism that they want to convert.

My advice is, *Be happy with the way God created you.* At Jewish Voice, we are not trying to convert people from one culture to another. Instead, we're trying to work within the framework of their culture and lead them to *the way, the truth the life.* (John 14:6)

2. *Church* is another word that has a negative connotation for Jews

Church is a word that stands for *the other religion.* I greatly prefer *believer, follower of Yeshua,* even *follower of Jesus.* Church comes from the Greek and has no Hebrew origins. It's a fine word in and of itself, which means *the called out ones.* But it is so completely identified with Christianity that it tends to raise a red flag in the Jewish mind.

3. *Baptize* is also a very difficult word

I don't deal with it until the person is a little more open. Even though immersion by water is an ancient Jewish idea, it has come to be identified so clearly with Christianity that it, too, can be a red flag.

4. *Christ*

When I was a boy, whenever I heard, "Christ," I thought of the son of Mr. and Mrs. Christ, the god of Christianity. I know that sounds ridiculous, but this is what the term brings to mind for many Jews of all ages. Like *church*, *Christ* is a Greek word that means *anointed one*. I prefer to use *Messiah*, which is closer to the Hebrew and means the very same thing. And, of course, I want Jewish People to know that His actual name given from Heaven is Yeshua. In Matthew 1:21, when the angel says *You shall call His name Jesus,* you lose the profound richness if you don't understand that *Yeshua,* the actual name given, means *salvation*.

5. *Cross*

Be careful not to over-emphasize the cross when you talk to a Jewish person about the Gospel.

Some may ask, "How is it possible to over-emphasize the cross?"

I don't mean to imply that we can ever talk too much about what Yeshua did for us on the cross. When Yeshua was on that cross, he took on the sins of the entire world and shed the blood that cleanses us from unrighteousness.

But we can go overboard if we turn the cross itself into an object of worship. That cross had no magical power. God did not miraculously preserve it so believers could bring it out on Easter and bow down to it.

For Jews the cross as a symbol can bring to mind thoughts of the Crusaders, marching toward Jerusalem — the cross on display at the front of their armies as they massacred Jewish communities along the way.

It serves as a reminder of uniforms worn by Nazi soldiers, which had a cross on it, implying that, "We kill you because you killed Jesus Christ." In fact, some Jews were marched into gas chambers under signs that read, "You are being killed in the name of Jesus Christ." Horrible, but true.

The Messianic Jewish version of the Bible, which was translated by my good friend David Stern replaces *cross* with *execution stake* or *tree*, which is consistent with prophecy and the Greek references in many cases. Messianic Jews will often say "tree." I'm not afraid to talk about the cross, but I want to make clear what it *doesn't* mean.

Of course, I want to respect Christians who place great value on the symbol of the cross, but I want to be sensitive to both sides.

What about the DOs?

We've talked quite a bit about the DON'Ts of witnessing to Jews. What about the DOs?

1. Learn to share the Gospel from the Old Testament

One of the best ways you can talk to Jewish People about Yeshua is to share the Gospel from the Old Testament.

It has been said, and rightly so, that the New Testament is concealed in the Old Testament and the Old Testament is revealed in the New.

The Old Testament is the story of man's sin and resulting separation from God. Beginning with the first chapters of Genesis, on through to the last sentence in the Book of Malachi, it clearly shows our need for a Redeemer and sets the stage for His arrival.

In Luke 24:27, Jesus pointed to Old Testament Scriptures to prove He was the Messiah. Acts 28:23 says that the apostles expounded the Scriptures to show that Jesus was the promised Messiah. Remember that there was no New Testament for them to use. After all, they wrote the New Testament! They were using the Jewish Scriptures to prove that Yeshua was exactly who He claimed to be — and you can do the same with a little study.

Don't forget that the Old Testament can be common ground for Christians and Jews who believe the Hebrew Scriptures are the inspired Word of God.

There are many references to Yeshua throughout the Hebrew Scriptures. The virgin birth. His rejection by His People. His atoning death on the cross.

One word of warning, though. Don't expect Jewish People to know the Old Testament. Most of them don't. Especially not here in America. The most recent statistics I've seen indicate that only about 10 percent of all Jews are actively involved in reading and studying the Bible. Most Jews who reject Yeshua as the Messiah haven't done so because of anything they've read or studied on their own. They reject Him because they've been told that you can't be

Jewish and believe in Jesus. They don't know why. They just do as they're told.

2. Some Scriptures you can use

Are there some particular Scriptures that can help open Jewish eyes to the divinity of Yeshua?

Yes, there are. One of my favorites asks:

> Who has gone up to heaven
> and come down?
> Who has gathered up the wind
> in the hollow of His hands?
> Who has wrapped up the waters
> in His cloak?
> Who has established all the ends
> of the earth?
> What is His name, and the name
> of His son?
> Tell me if you know!
> (Proverbs 30:4)

This passage is obviously referring to God and says clearly that He has a Son.

Then, of course, there is Isaiah 53, the passage my friend Sid Roth read to his father. This Scripture refers to the One who *took up our infirmities and carried our sorrows*, reminding us that He *was pierced for our transgressions, He was crushed for our iniquities.* (Isaiah 53:4-5)

Psalm 22 is another very good passage, with its portrayal of the crucifixion. It's impossible to read that Scripture with an open mind and not be moved by its depiction of the suffering Yeshua endured as He died for the sins of mankind.

3. Jewish objections to Yeshua

Now one of the biggest objections Jewish People have with regard to Yeshua is His claim of divinity. They'll tell you that there are no passages in the Old Testament to indicate the Messiah will be anything more than a man.

He'll be a special man, they say. He'll be anointed, but he won't be divine.

They also object to teachings on the Trinity and say that Christians believe in three gods, while Jews believe in only one.

And yet, right in the first chapter of Genesis, the Creator says,

> Let *Us* make man in *Our* own image, in *Our* likeness. . . (Genesis 1:26, emphasis added).

(I must say, though, that I like to refer to the Father, Son and Spirit as the Tri-Unity rather than the Trinity. I think it is a better expression of the reality.)

Another good passage to overcome Jewish objections to Yeshua is the fifth chapter of Micah, which refers to a ruler *whose origins are from of old:*

"But you, Bethlehem Ephrathah,
though you are small among the clans of Judah,
out of you will come for Me
One who will be Ruler over Israel,
whose origins are from of old,
from ancient times."
Therefore Israel will be abandoned
until the time when she who is in
labor gives birth
and the rest of His brothers return
to join the Israelites.
He will stand and shepherd His flock
in the strength of the LORD,
in the majesty of the name of the
LORD His God.
And they will lie securely,
for then His greatness
will reach to the ends of the earth.
And He will be their peace.
(Micah 5:2-5)

And how about:

For to us a Child is born,
to us a Son is given,
and the government will be on His shoulders.
And He will be called

> Wonderful Counselor, Mighty God,
> Everlasting Father, Prince of Peace.
> (Isaiah 9:6)

How can you deny that this passage is speaking about Someone who is of divine origin? You can't!

I also like to point to the 31ˢᵗ chapter of Jeremiah, which we've already discussed in some detail. This passage in verse 34 talks about God's new covenant with the People of Israel, one in which He *will remember their sins no more*. Here again is a reference to the grace God offers through the atoning sacrifice of His Son.

4. They don't care what you know, until . . .

Here's another great way to reach the Jewish People for Yeshua: Show them His love.

I'm sure you've heard the old saying, "People don't care how much you know until they know how much you care."

This is the absolute truth.

Our Lord's brother, author of the Book of James, addresses this when he writes,

> Suppose a brother or sister is without clothes
> and daily food. If one of you says to him, "Go,
> I wish you well; keep warm and well fed," but
> does nothing about his physical needs, what
> good is it? (James 2:15-16)

The Apostle John asks,

> If anyone has material possessions and sees his
> brother in need but has no pity on him, how
> can the love of God be in him? Dear children,
> let us not love with words or tongue but with
> actions and in truth. (1 John 3:17-18)

One of the ways we at Jewish Voice share our faith is by
operating medical clinics where we provide essential medi-
cines, eyeglasses, dental care and more. Last year, we supplied medical care for more than 7,500 people — the vast
majority of the needy Jews — in countries like Ethiopia.

**About 80 percent of those we helped were
willing to go into our prayer lines, and 606
of them made commitments to the Lord
and were given audio Bibles.** (Some 600
of these were Jewish, and the other six were
Muslims.)

As we reach out with God's love, we often find that He
confirms His Word with signs and wonders. This is what
happened in 2007 in the district of Gondar in Ethiopia,
where we were helping people who have been living in total
squalor in refugee camps.

To give you a little background, these are people of Jewish
ancestry who are hoping to make their aliyah (return to Israel)

under the Law of Return. One of their biggest problems is that they are extremely poor, and it will be a struggle for Israel to assimilate them. (One of every three Israelis lives in poverty, and the country is understandably reluctant to bring in more families who will need assistance.) Some of these Ethiopian Jews have been living in camps for 20 years. They have almost nothing except the clothes they wear.

Although the elders of the community are happy to have us come in and provide help for their people, they are also wary because they don't want to be *tainted* by associating with Christians. They fear this would be another reason for the Israeli government to refuse to take them in.

One of those who came to us for help last year was a young man in his late teens who had been deaf and mute his entire life. He had never uttered a single word. Nor had he ever heard one.

Medically, there was nothing we could do to restore his hearing and speech. But we could, and did, pray for him.

And when we did, God gave a miracle.

It's impossible to describe the amazed look on his face when he began to hear other people's voices. Imagine being nearly 20 years old and having never heard a sound in your life. At first, his eyes bugged out as if he was terrified. And then, when he realized what was going on, his face lit up with a huge grin.

I felt like I was living out the Book of Acts. The elders of that community had known that young man his entire life.

There was no denying that he had been deaf, and now he could hear.

Some of those elders were sitting in the waiting room at the clinic when that young man came out of the prayer room, praising God for his healing.

I whispered, "Yeshua," into his ear and he repeated it clearly.

Then I stood beside him and said, "Yeshua, Shalom."

Again, he repeated what I said without hesitation.

Then, as he and his parents wept together for joy, I walked over to the elders and asked, "What do you think of this?"

They looked at each other and briefly discussed the situation in Amharic, their native tongue. After a moment, one of the men turned back to me and said in perfect English, "We don't know what to think of this."

I wasn't giving up that easily.

"What are you going to do about it?" I asked.

"We don't know what to do." They just couldn't deal with it.

But no matter what they said to me, or how much they might try to deny it, I knew that those Ethiopian Jews had seen Yeshua's power. They can no longer deny His power or His mercy. Seeds have been planted that will eventually produce an abundant harvest of souls.

Chapter Ten

A STEP FURTHER

"I will make you into a great nation
and I will bless you;
I will make your name great,
and you will be a blessing.
I will bless those who bless you,
and whoever curses you I will curse;
and all peoples on earth
will be blessed through you."
(Genesis 12:2-3)

In the latter days of the 15th century, Spain was the world's pre-eminent power. Christopher Columbus sailed to the New World under the Spanish flag, and Spain quickly gained a foothold there.

But it was also during this time that Spain turned against the Jews.

Thousands of Jews were forcibly expelled from the country, and many more were tortured and killed during the Spanish Inquisition.

And almost immediately, Spain's fortunes began to decline. With the utter destruction of the Spanish Armada less than 100 years later, Spain's fall from power was complete.

Was this an example of Genesis 12 at work? It would seem so.

Consider what happened to Germany during and after World War II. Hitler murdered 6 million Jews. In doing so, he brought on a war that killed 7 million German citizens and left behind a devastated, divided country.

Radio personality Dennis Prager writes, "Look at who most blesses the Jews and who most curses them, and you decide whether the verse in Genesis has validity." He goes on to say, "It is the Arab world that curses the Jews. It rivals Nazi Germany for the ubiquity and intensity of its Jew-hatred. Look at its state. According to Arab scholars, appointed by the United Nations to report on the state of Arab society, that part of the world lags behind the rest of humanity, including in most instances sub-Saharan Africa, in virtually every social, moral and intellectual indicator. And there is no question but that its half-century long preoccupation with destroying Israel has only increased the Arab world's woes." [26]

My friend Bill Koenig wrote a book called *Eye to Eye*,[27] in which he presents compelling evidence that the fortunes of the United States are clearly tied to our treatment of Israel — and specifically to our defense of Israel's right to the Land God promised her. The bottom line is that every time we pressure Israel to give up land in exchange for peace, something terrible happens. It seems that God expects us to take

His covenants seriously. Here is a small sampling of what Bill's research uncovered:

October 20, 1991

As the first President Bush opens the Madrid Conference, which will ask Israel to give up land in return for peace in the Middle East, a huge storm develops in the North Atlantic. The storm travels 1,000 miles from east to west (the opposite of what normally happens), and sends 35-foot waves crashing onto the New England coast — including President Bush's home at Kennebunkport, Maine.

August 23, 1992

When the Madrid Conference moves to Washington, D.C., Hurricane Andrew storms ashore in Florida, leaving behind an estimated $30 million in damage.

January 16, 1994

President Bill Clinton meets with Syria's President Hafez el-Assad in Geneva, and the two talk about a peace agreement with Israel that involves giving the Golan Heights back to Palestinian control. The next day, the Northridge Earthquake hits Southern California — at the time, the second most destructive natural disaster in America's history (behind only Hurricane Andrew).

September 28, 1998

As Secretary of State Madeline Albright works out the final details of a peace agreement that would ask Israel to give up 13 percent of Judea and Samaria, Hurricane George slams into the Gulf Coast. Final tally of the destruction: $1 billion.

October 15-22, 1998

Another $1 billion disaster hits America when Palestine Liberation Organization Chairman Yasser Arafat meets with Israeli Prime Minister Benjamin Netanyahu in Maryland. The topic, once again, is Israel's willingness to give up land for peace. This time, the state of Texas is hit by a series of tornadoes and torrential rainstorms.

There are so many similar examples to choose from, but here are just a few more:

May 3, 1999

On the day Yasser Arafat is scheduled to declare a Palestinian state with Jerusalem as its capital — with the blessing of the United States government — the most powerful tornados on record wreak havoc in Oklahoma and Kansas, with winds recorded at more than 300 miles an hour. Arafat agrees to postpone his declaration until December, at the request of President Clinton.

October 11, 1999

On the day when Israelis in 15 West Bank communities are evicted from their land, America is rocked by a series of disasters. First, the Dow falls 266 points, its worst loss in 10 years. Then a hurricane slams into North Carolina. A few days later, a 7.1 earthquake shakes the southwestern desert.

August 2005

Jewish families are evicted from their homes in the Gaza Strip as part of Prime Minister Ariel Sharon's *Disengagement Plan* for the region. Sharon's agreement to this plan came largely as the result of pressure from the Bush Administration. As Americans watching television saw what was happening in the Middle East, news bulletins reported that a hurricane was forming in the Atlantic. The name, they said, was Katrina.

Am I saying that God killed all those innocent people along the Gulf Coast to teach the United States a lesson? Not at all. I don't think for a moment that God sent these calamities upon the American people. Instead, I believe He merely lifted his hand of protection, and we were battered by one disaster after another. Who knows what would happen every day if God was not protecting us? We'll never know how many times He has stretched out His hand to protect us, individually and as a nation.

One way we can ensure His continued blessing and protection is to bless the People of Israel.

We are called to bless the Jews

I believe it's clear that everyone who believes in Yeshua is called to do everything he or she can to bless the Jewish People. There are many reasons for this, beginning with the fact that the Messiah Himself was a Jew by birth.

We also owe the Jews a debt of gratitude because they preserved the Old Testament Scriptures — and because all 27 books of the New Testament were written by Jews.

But most of all, Gentile believers are called to bless Jews because God said, "I will bless those who bless you."

One question I'm often asked is, "Do you believe that, as a Christian, I am obligated to unequivocally support every action taken by the State of Israel?"

Absolutely not! As a Jew myself, I understand that the Jewish People are not perfect. The government of Israel is not acting as God's infallible agent. The Israeli government can and does make decisions that should be criticized.

The one thing we must understand about the country of Israel is that it has a biblical land grant to the territory within its borders.

If we look at Israel through God's eyes, we will see that they have a right to the Land. This doesn't mean that God loves the Jew more than the Arab, but that He made an everlasting decree to give this Land to the descendants of Abraham, Isaac, and Jacob.

I'm not relying on one or two isolated passages of Scripture to support my view on this. There are numerous verses that refer to Israel's eternal right to the Land:

"All the land that you see I will give to you and your offspring forever." (Genesis 13:15)

"Remember your servants Abraham, Isaac and Israel, to whom You swore by Your own self: *'I will make your descendants as numerous as the stars in the sky and I will give your descendants all this land I promised them, and it will be their inheritance forever.'"* (Exodus 32:13)

"So on that day Moses swore to me, *'The Land on which your feet have walked will be your inheritance and that of your children forever, because you have followed the* LORD *my God wholeheartedly.'"* (Joshua 14:9)

"O our God, did You not drive out the inhabitants of this land before Your people Israel and give it forever to the descendants of Abraham Your friend?" (2 Chronicles 20:7)

There are also many passages that call believers from all nations to bless the People of Israel. One of them is:

For if the Gentiles have shared in the Jews' spiritual blessings, they owe it to the Jews to share with them their material blessings. (Romans 15:27)

How can we share our blessings with the People of Israel? Here are a few ways:

1. Support ministries that are preaching the Gospel to the Jewish People

There are several good organizations that do this, including Jewish Voice, the organization I serve as President.

But before you make a donation to one of these organizations, I urge you to do some investigating to make certain that your money is going where you want it to go. How much of what you give will go directly into ministry and how much will be spent on overhead, fundraising or other costs? Go online and check out the organization's mission statement. Who is endorsing them? Do they have approval from watchdog groups such as the Better Business Bureau, the Evangelical Council of Financial Accountability, or Charity Navigator?

I'm not trying to be negative. I just want to make sure that your financial contributions go exactly where you want them to go — that they are used to bless the Jewish People both financially and spiritually. Unfortunately, there are organizations that give the appearance of being evangelical but are not.

They raise a great deal of money from evangelical Christians; but if you read their materials closely, you will see that they do not accept Yeshua as Messiah and Lord. Although much of the money these groups raise goes to worthwhile causes, I have heard that some of it eventually finds its way into support for anti-missionary groups. In other words, Christians' dollars are being spent to fight the spread of the

Gospel and even to persecute Jewish believers and counter Messianic ministries living and working in Israel.

I think the first responsibility of Christians is to be concerned about the Household of Faith in Israel, or to support ministries that are reaching the Jewish People, and bringing aid to Jewish communities in need.

When the Apostle Paul took offerings, it was for the suffering believers in Jerusalem. That seems to be lost on the Christian Zionist community. I know of one high-profile Christian organization that has sent a great deal of financial support to an ultra-orthodox orphanage. Although I'm always in favor of helping hurting children — and especially orphans — I also know that the ultra-orthodox Jews have a very clear agenda to rid Israel of what they see as *the missionary threat* — and that includes expelling from the Land all who believe in Yeshua.

Again, we have to be very careful regarding where our money goes. Christians have to understand that there is a great deal of persecution of Messianic Jews in Israel. I have heard story after story of believers having lost their jobs, their homes and, basically being marked as outcasts. In fact, Jewish Voice is involved in litigation in Israel right now on behalf of a bakery whose owners lost their kosher license simply because it was discovered that they are believers.

So you can see that we need to pray and work for change in Israel.

Now more than ever before, as God's plan for the Last Days is carried out, Jews in Israel are receptive to hearing the Good News of Yeshua. And, as Jewish hearts turn to our Messiah, the time for His return will come closer and closer. I know that the last thing any believer would want to do is invest his or her money in an effort to *prevent* Jews from hearing the Gospel.

So again, give generously. But give carefully.

2. Support charities that are providing food, clothing and other services to Jews who live in poverty

Many Jews around the world live in horrible poverty. In the former Soviet Union, many thousands of Jews are homeless, or very close to it. Large extended families are crammed into tiny apartments where children may sleep three or four (or more) to a bed. Often, such families have to choose between essentials such as food, heating during the long, cold winter, and paying the rent.

In many countries, Jewish poverty is perpetuated by anti-Semitism that blocks the doors to good employment, denies entrance to the best schools and, basically, keeps the Jewish People marginalized and in need.

Tragically, many families that immigrate to Israel find that the situation is not much better there. Constant terrorist attacks against Israel have forced the Israeli government to greatly increase defense spending, thus forcing drastic budget cuts in social programs.

Unemployment is high and one-third of the Israeli People live below the poverty line. I know it breaks God's heart to see His People living this way, and He wants us to do what we can to help them. He calls out to us in Isaiah 40:1: *'Comfort, comfort my people...'*

Yes, do what you can to help the People of Israel. But please make sure that your dollars are going to support organizations that are committed to reaching Jewish People with the Gospel, and providing help for Messianic Jews living in poverty.

I know of one organization that raises millions of dollars every year to help impoverished Jews in Israel and the former Soviet Union. Virtually all of that money comes from evangelical Christians. In fact, the leader of that particular group regularly speaks in Christian churches across the country. And yet, he writes:

> The notion that Jews are damned without Christ and that only through him and Christianity can they find fulfillment is utterly rejected.

And:

> A Jew who accepts Jesus as Lord or Messiah effectively ceases to be a Jew... He is like a defector who walked out on his God and his family.

And then there's this little tidbit:

> From a Jewish point of view, Messianic Jews are a front for Evangelical Christians who try

to wean Jews away from their ancestral faith by lulling them into believing that they can accept Jesus as Lord and still remain Jewish. [28]

Would you want your dollars to go to an organization whose leader holds these beliefs? I certainly wouldn't!

3. Support Messianic organizations who are helping Jews make Aliyah to Israel

What an exciting thing it is to be able to partner with God in the unfolding of His plan for Creation.

In these thrilling days, God is working through believers like you and me to fulfill the prophecy He first gave in Deuteronomy:

> "...and when you and your children return to the LORD your God and obey Him with all your heart and with all your soul... then the LORD your God will restore your fortunes and have compassion on you and gather you again from all the nations where He scattered you." (Deuteronomy 30:2-3)

Already 1 million Jews have made Aliyah — returned to Israel — from the former Soviet Union. Thousands of Ethiopian Jews have returned as well. Others have come from Argentina and countries in South America. The number of

Jews returning to Israel is rapidly increasing as we move toward our Messiah's return.

As we've already seen, the return of Jews to the Holy Land is a clear and, I believe, undeniable sign that the Last Days are here.

But satan is hard at work trying to stop it from happening. He is especially concerned about keeping Messianic Jews out of Israel, for two reasons. First, because he hates it when anyone comes to Yeshua. And second, because he knows that Messianic Jews will share their faith, which means that other Jews will be won to Messiah, and His return will come ever closer.

Here's just one example of the trouble our ancient enemy is stirring up.

The Israeli Supreme Court recently ruled that Jews who *convert to another religion* — in their view, Jews who accept Yeshua as Messiah — are no longer Jewish and are therefore ineligible for citizenship under the Law of Return. It's so important for Christians in America to stand up and fight this law. The government of Israel knows that they have no better friend than America's Evangelical Christians. Your opinion is valued and will be heard.

It would help so much if you would send a card or e-mail to the Israeli government, letting it be known that you believe Messianic Jews should be allowed to return to Israel under the Law of Return.

It doesn't make sense to me that you can be just about anything else and be allowed back into Israel.

"You're an atheist? Fine, come on in."

"You're a Hare Krishna, but your mother was a Jew? No problem."

"Gay? Welcome to Israel."

"You say you've come to believe in Yeshua as Messiah? Sorry, we don't want your kind here."

I believe there is a very real danger that the Israeli government will kick out all missionaries. There have already been instances when someone's citizenship was revoked because it was discovered that he was a believer.

From a natural point of view, the policy of the Israeli government makes absolutely no sense. But put satan into the mix, and it's easy to see exactly what's going on.

So again, is it important to help Jews return to Israel from the countries where they've been scattered? Absolutely. But again, be careful and prayerful when it comes to choosing which organizations you should support.

4. Provoke the Jews to jealousy

What does it mean to provoke the Jews to jealousy?

It means to make them want what you have. And, of course, what you have is eternal life through faith in the Son of God.

You know, it's not against our sin nature to want to make other people jealous. It's part of our basic instinct, and something that most of us have tried to fight at one time or another.

Let's be completely honest:

It's perfectly *natural* to want people to be jealous of the car we drive.

It makes us feel good if people see where we live and say, "Wow, I wish that was my house!" We want people to be envious of our job, our popularity, our intelligence, our designer clothing, our membership in exclusive clubs or any of hundreds of other things. That's why people will spend hundreds, or even thousands of dollars, for a purse that has a designer name attached to it.

Now, when I say *purse*, I'm not picking on women. I could have just as easily said *necktie*. But the point I'm making is that a purse is just a purse. You can get one at Target that functions just as well as the one you buy on Rodeo Drive in Beverly Hills. But if you do get one at Barney's, your friends will say, "Oh, that's such a cool purse. I wish I had one like it."

We don't even realize it, but much of what we do stems from our desire to make other people jealous.

God grant us the grace to be as proud of our relationship with Him as we are of the purses we carry or the clothes we wear!

It's time we stopped being embarrassed to talk to others about the Gospel, and, instead, start flaunting the fact that we have something that everyone would want for themselves if they could see how good it is.

That's exactly what Paul is talking about when he says,

> I make much of my ministry in the hope that
> I may somehow arouse my own people to envy

and save some of them. (Romans 11:13-14)

You will provoke Jewish People to envy when they see how you handle yourself in the midst of a crisis, experiencing the grace of God and the peace that passes understanding.

They will be provoked to jealousy when they see that you have a living relationship with the very God who chose them as His People and led them out of slavery in Egypt.

Jesus said that nobody lights a lamp and then hides it under a bowl. Then He added,

> "In the same way, let your light shine before men." (Matthew 5:16)

Let God's light shine through you at all times. Those who see the joy and love in you will be envious — even those who are Jews. And this is one time when envy is a good thing.

5. Pray for the Jewish People and for peace in the Middle East

Are you praying for the Jewish People? If not, will you please make it a point to do so? You can stand with the Apostle Paul, who says,

> Brothers, my heart's desire and prayer to God
> for the Israelites is that they may be saved.
> (Romans 10:1)

Psalm 122:6 also says, *Pray for the peace of Jerusalem.*
Thank you for praying:

- That Jewish People around the world will come to know Yeshua as Messiah and Lord.
- That God will protect His People from satan, who seeks to destroy them.
- That He will provide food, shelter and comfort for Jews — especially children and the elderly — who are living in horrible poverty.
- That Yeshua will make His love known to Jews who deal with anti-Semitism and persecution on a daily basis.
- For special protection over those who live in areas of Israel that are especially vulnerable to terrorist attacks.
- And for those in authority in Israel, that they might seek the Lord in the decisions they make.

6. Understand your Jewish heritage

How much do you know about your spiritual heritage?

It's sad, but many evangelical believers know almost nothing about the history of the Christian religion. They seem to think that the American Church mirrors first century Christianity — and don't have an understanding of the Jewish roots of their faith.

I've already talked about how surprised I was when I read the New Testament for the very first time. I had no idea that Christians believed in the same God to whom I'd always prayed. I didn't know they honored the same heroes I'd learned about in synagogue — Abraham, Moses, Noah, David, Elijah and many others, all of whom were Jewish. How thrilled I was to discover that Jesus Himself was a Jew!

I was delighted and amazed to see the clear, strong connection between Judaism and Christianity. Today, I pray that more Christians will discover that connection. I believe that if more Christians understand and honor the Jewish roots of their faith, it will open the door to greater dialogue with Jewish People. And that, in turn, will lead to more Jews experiencing a life-changing encounter with our risen Lord.

Let me ask you a question: How do you picture Jesus as a child?

Close your eyes and think about it for a moment.

Do you see Him as an archetypical Roman Catholic altar boy — straight off the cover of the latest Hallmark Christmas card?

Do you see him sitting in a Sunday school class at the neighborhood mega-church, a blonde-haired, blue-eyed tyke who would look at home in a Norman Rockwell painting?

Do you see Him as He was — a Jew who followed Jewish customs and observed Jewish Feast Days? Do you know how His family kept the Sabbath? When did they attend synagogue, and what did they do there when they did? What rituals did they follow in their daily life? What Feasts did they celebrate? And why and how did they celebrate them?

If you know the answers to the questions I'm asking, then find someone to give you the pat on the back you deserve.

If you don't know the answers, then it might be time to invest a little time in studying the Jewish roots of Christianity.

The Jews of the first century who put their faith in Yeshua never meant to start a religious movement that was separate and distinct from Judaism. The expectation was that the Jewish Nation would turn to Yeshua en masse, and for awhile it seemed that was going to happen. Thousands were coming to faith every single day.

These early believers continued to worship in the Temple. They circumcised their children and followed the Jewish dietary laws.

The Apostle Paul went to the synagogue every Sabbath, even when he was on his missionary trips to take the Gospel to the Gentiles. (See Acts 18:4, for example.)

It was only when opposition grew, and the Jewish believers were no longer welcome in the synagogue that Christianity crystallized into a separate movement.

For hundreds of years after that, Jewish People were told that they couldn't follow Yeshua and maintain their Jewish identity.

As early as 150 years after the birth of Yeshua, Justin Martyr wrote to Trypho the Jew, telling him, "You can be a Jew or a Christian, but you can't be both."

And that's pretty much how it's been.

Jews who accepted Yeshua were expected to leave the Jewish culture behind and fit into the Christian Church.

It is only within the last 100 years or so that this began to change when Jews who had come to faith in Yeshua asked,

"Why should I have to give up my cultural heritage?"

Why indeed? There is nothing *unchristian* about worshiping on the Sabbath, wearing a tallit or observing Passover.

There's no reason why a Jewish believer should act like a *Christian*.

Nor is there any reason why a Christian should act like a Jewish believer. If you're a Gentile Christian, you can get in touch with your Jewish roots without wearing a skull cap and a tallit or blowing a shofar.

Yes, it bothers me when I see Gentiles trying to act like Jews. The Bible says,

> There is neither Jew nor Greek, slave nor free,
> male nor female, for you are all one in Christ
> Jesus. (Galatians 3:28)

That doesn't mean we all have to start behaving one way. I'm a man and I act like a man. My wife is a woman and she acts like a woman. But there is no difference between us with regard to our position in Messiah.

I'm a Jew by birth and in many ways I act like a Jew. Your heritage may be English, French, German, African. Whatever, it's perfectly fine for you to be proud of your heritage and demonstrate that in your daily life.

My point is that God made us all the way we are. The best thing we can do is accept that, enjoy it, and appreciate the diversity that God has built into His creation.

I'm sure you've heard it said, *bloom where you're planted.*

Today, an increasing number of Jews are *blooming* through faith in Yeshua. And because of that, the whole world is about to change forever.

Chapter Eleven

JESUS AND ISRAEL

When I first came to saving faith in Yeshua, I was amazed to
see how His life reflected the history of Israel.

Or, to put it more accurately, I was amazed to see how
the history of Israel reflected the life of Messiah.

If you've ever been to the Capitol Mall in Washington,
D.C., you are familiar with the Reflecting Pool between
the Lincoln Memorial and the Washington Monument.
On a bright summer's day, the reflection in that pool is so
clear it will almost make you think there's a building down
in that water.

But of course, there isn't. It's only a reflection.

I have discovered that looking at the history of Israel is
like looking into a reflection of Yeshua Himself. Many events
that took place in Israel's history foreshadowed what would
happen later on in the life of Yeshua. For example:

- The Children of Israel journeyed to Egypt to escape
  certain death at the hands of famine. (Genesis 42:1-
  47:12)

- Yeshua and His family fled into Egypt to escape certain death at the hands of Herod. (Matthew 2:13-18)

- The Israelites were *baptized* in the Red Sea as they fled from the Egyptian army. (Exodus 14:10-13)
- Jesus was baptized by John the Baptist at the start of His earthly ministry. (Matthew 3:13-17)

- The Jewish Nation wandered in the wilderness for 40 years on their way to the Promised Land. (Exodus 16:1-17:7)
- Yeshua spent 40 days in the wilderness, being tempted by satan, before He began His earthly ministry. (Matthew 4:1-11)

- Moses went up a mountain (Mt. Sinai) to get the Ten Commandments from God. (Exodus 19:1-23:33)
- Yeshua delivered His most famous sermon from a mountain (the Mount of Olives), during which He pronounced the ten blessings known as The Beatitudes. (Matthew chapters 5 through 7)

- When Moses came down from the Mountain after getting the Ten Commandments, His face was shining with the Glory of God. (Exodus 34:29-35)
- When Yeshua went up on the Mount of Transfiguration, *His face shone like the sun.* (Matthew 17:2)

There are, of course, many other comparisons. The blood of the animals sacrificed by the Israelites was only a very pale substitute for the blood of the Lamb (Yeshua), which was shed to take away the sins of all mankind.

And then, too, there was the idea of the scapegoat, who carried the sins of the People into the wilderness. (Leviticus 16:10) Yeshua was the true Scapegoat, who took our punishment upon Himself, even though He had done nothing wrong.

The Messiah's life is also mirrored in a very important way in the seven *mo'adim, appointed times,* or Festivals of the Hebrew calendar. Four of these — the Spring Feasts, refer to events that occurred during Messiah's earthly ministry. The other three — the Fall Feasts, refer to events that are about to happen when He comes for the second time.

To the Israelites, each one of these holy days was known as a *mikrah,* which means *rehearsal* or *recital.* Paul tells us that all of these special days have been appointed by God to reveal the Messiah to the world as part of God's great plan for His creation:

> Therefore do not let anyone judge you by what you eat or drink, or with regard to a religious festival, a New Moon celebration or a Sabbath day. These are a shadow of the things that were to come; the reality, however, is found in Christ. (Colossians 2:16-17)

The four celebrations which take place during the spring of the year are called *former rain* festivals. Yeshua was the personal fulfillment of every one of them, beginning with:

Passover

To non-Jews, this is probably the best-known of the Biblical Feasts. Any Christian who is the least bit familiar with the Old Testament will certainly understand the connection between Passover and the sacrificial death of the Messiah.

You remember how Moses went to Pharaoh and asked him to free the Israelite People, who had become slaves in Egypt. When the Egyptian leader refused to listen, God sent a number of plagues on the land of Egypt, including an infestation of frogs, swarms of locusts, blood, hail, and darkness.

The Egyptians suffered terribly, but Pharaoh would still not let the Israelites leave Egypt.

Finally, God told Moses that every Hebrew family was to sacrifice a lamb without defect. After the lamb had been killed, some of its blood was to be placed on the top and two sides of the doorframe of their house. (Notice that the blood was to be applied in the shape of a cross.) At midnight on the specified day, the Lord struck down every firstborn child in Egypt who lived in a house that was not sprinkled with the blood of a lamb. The houses belonging to the Israelites were *passed over*, thus the name of Passover was set aside to commemorate this great occasion in the history of Israel — the event that finally brought their freedom.

God commanded that all future generations sacrifice the Passover lamb in springtime on the 14th of Aviv. The festival always included a public sacrifice of a national Passover lamb. As the lamb was led to its death, crowds of people would line the streets of Jerusalem, singing joyously as they remembered their ancestors' delivery from Egypt. One passage that was sung came from Psalm 118:

> O LORD save us; O LORD grant us success.
> Blessed is he who comes in the name of the
> LORD. (Psalm 118:25-26)

It was during Passover week that Jesus made His final entrance into Jerusalem, following the same route that the Passover lamb had taken. Crowds placed palm branches in front of Him and celebrated as He passed, riding on a donkey to show that He was coming in humility and peace.

For four days, the Passover lamb was to be kept in public view so that anyone who wished to examine the animal could do so, ensuring that the animal was without defect as commanded. While this was going on, the Pharisees and Sadducees were trying desperately to find fault with Yeshua, but could not do so. In fact, Pontius Pilate, who agreed to have the Messiah executed, washed his hands in front of the crowd and told them, *I am innocent of this man's blood. It is your responsibility.* (Matthew 27:24)

There are many more parallels between the death of Yeshua and the sacrifice of the Passover lamb.

- The blood stains on the Savior's head, hands and feet matched the blood placed on the door frame of every Israeli house in Egypt.
- It was forbidden for any of the Passover lamb's bones to be broken (Exodus 12:46) and, similarly, none of Messiah's bones were broken, although Roman soldiers did break the legs of the two thieves who were crucified on either side of Him. (John 19:31-37)
- According to some Bible historians, the Passover lamb was sacrificed about 3 p.m., the same time when Yeshua cried out in a loud voice and died. (Matthew 27:45-50)

The Feast of Unleavened Bread

This feast begins the day after Passover ends, and lasts for seven days. Over the years, it has gradually been incorporated into Passover.

At the beginning of this celebration, the woman of the house goes through her home, sprinkling breadcrumbs in every room — especially in hard-to-reach areas. Then she goes back through with a broom, sweeping all of that *leaven* (yeast) back into the kitchen. This pile of bread crumbs is then taken out into the yard and burned.

To the Jews, yeast has always represented sin or evil. They understood that a little sin can impact every aspect of a person's life, just as a little yeast impacts an entire loaf of bread. That's why Yeshua told His disciples, *Be on your guard against the yeast of the Pharisees and Sadducees.* (Matthew 16:11)

What does this have to do with the Messiah? Simply this: He is the only Person to ever live who has not been contaminated by the yeast of evil that abounds in our world. Because He had not been corrupted by sin, His body would not decay in the grave. There was to be no decomposition of His flesh.

The Feast of Unleavened Bread proclaims that the Savior's physical body would not experience the ravages of death — and that it is through His own sinless nature that we can be spared from the consequences of our own sin. This feast also serves to remind us that we must be yielded to Him in order that He can purge us of harmful leaven and put our feet on the road to eternal life.

The Feast of Firstfruits

This feast, also called the Omer, is described in Leviticus 23:9-14. When his barley crop was ready to be harvested, the Hebrew farmer would bring his first sheaf to the priest, who would literally wave it before the Lord. It was a reminder to the Israelites that they were to put God first in every area of their lives.

It was also during this festival that first-born children and animals were presented to the Lord.

This feast points toward Yeshua who is:

- God's first-born. (Hebrews 1:6)
- Mary's first-born. (Matthew 1:23-25)
- The first to rise from the dead. (Acts 26:23)
- The firstborn among many brothers. (Romans 8:29)

- The beginning and the firstborn from among the dead. (Colossians 1:18)

Another important aspect of this feast is its focus on resurrection. The winter months, when the fields were barren and empty, have passed. Warm weather returns to the land and new life appears everywhere.

There is a clear and strong connection to the resurrection of Yeshua on the third day following His crucifixion.

Shavuot (The Feast of Weeks/Pentecost)

Shavuot is the final of the spring feasts. It is also called the Feast of Weeks because it takes place seven weeks and one day after the Feast of Firstfruits. In Leviticus, God says:

> "From the day after the Sabbath, the day you brought the sheaf of the wave offering, count off seven full weeks. Count off fifty days up to the day after the seventh Sabbath and then present an offering of new grain to the Lord." (Leviticus 23:15-16)

On this occasion, the Israelites brought two loaves of bread, containing yeast, which were presented to the Lord as a wave offering.

These two loaves of bread symbolically anticipated the time when both Jews and Gentiles would be made righteous — when we would be purged of leaven — through the blood of the lamb. In the second chapter of Ephesians, Paul says,

For He Himself is our peace, who has made the two one and has destroyed the barrier [between Gentiles and Jews], the dividing wall of hostility, by abolishing in His flesh the law with its commandments and regulations. His purpose was to create in Himself one new man out of the two, thus making peace, and in this one body to reconcile both of them to God through the cross, by which He put to death their hostility. (Ephesians 2:14-16)

Yeshua was crucified during Passover, on the very same day the Passover lamb was sacrificed. Then He rose from the dead on the day the Feast of Firstfruits was celebrated. Following that, He spent 40 days with His disciples before His ascension into Heaven. Just before He ascended, He told His disciples to wait in Jerusalem until they had been baptized with the Holy Spirit. (Acts 1:1-5)

This was fulfilled ten days later on Shavuot when the disciples were filled with the Holy Spirit *and began to speak in other tongues as the Spirit enabled them.* About 3,000 people came to faith in Yeshua that day (Acts 2:40-41) and the Church was born.

Purim

So far we've been talking specifically about feasts that take place in the spring of the year. But before we move on to talk about the fall feasts that will be fulfilled at the time of the Second Coming, I want to mention one important winter feast day that also points us toward the Messiah.

Purim is a joyous winter celebration that commemorates Queen Esther's heroic deliverance of the Jews from the plot of an evil politician named Haman. (We touched on this in Chapter 2.)

Esther is undoubtedly one of the great heroes in Jewish history. She put her own life on the line to rescue her People. But again, what she did is just a shadow of the redemption God had planned for His People. Esther brought a temporary reprieve from physical suffering and death. Yeshua's sacrificial death on the cross enabled the Jewish People — and every other people group on earth — to escape death forever.

Now I want to talk about three more feasts that are about to be fulfilled when Yeshua returns to earth to establish His Millennial Kingdom. These are:

- **Rosh Hashanah** (the Feast of Trumpets)
- **Yom Kippur** (the Day of Atonement)
- **Sukkot** (the Feast of Tabernacles)

Rosh Hashanah

In ancient Israel, a trumpet (or shofar) was blown for two important reasons. One was to announce an assembly of the people. The second was to sound an alarm and call the troops together to repel an enemy attack.

Rosh Hashanah, which means *head of the year*, is also known as the Feast of Trumpets. The trumpet blown on this holy day is a representation of the trumpet blast that will signify the end of the age.

Rosh Hashanah is surrounded by a 40-day season of repentance known as *Elul*. On each day of Elul, the trumpet is blown to remind the people to repent because Rosh Hashanah is approaching.

During this time, the religious leaders read to the people from the 27th Psalm and the 33rd chapter of Ezekiel. Psalm 27 is an encouragement to those who belong to God and are seeking to live in His will:

> For in the day of trouble He will keep me safe in His dwelling; He will hide me in the shelter of His tabernacle and set me high upon a rock. (Psalm 27:5)

Ezekiel 33, on the other hand, is a warning to those who do not heed the trumpet's call:

> 'When I bring the sword against a land, and the people of the land choose one of their men and make him their watchman, and he sees the sword coming against the land and blows the trumpet to warn the people, then if anyone hears the trumpet but does not take

warning and the sword comes and takes his life, his blood will be on his own head.' (Ezekiel 33:2-4)

I believe we are living in the time of Elul and God is calling us to repentance. The trumpet is about to sound, signifying our Messiah's return. Those who are living for Him long for this day and will see it as a wonderful time of joy and triumph. But those who are not right with God will experience terror and destruction.

The Prophet Zephaniah urges,

Seek the LORD, all you humble of the land, you who do what He commands. Seek righteousness, seek humility; perhaps you will be sheltered on the day of the LORD's anger. (Zephaniah 2:3)

The Old Testament prophet is talking about the same event to which Paul refers:

For the Lord Himself will come down from heaven, with a loud command, with the voice of the archangel and with the trumpet call of God, and the dead in Christ will rise first. After that, we who are still alive and are left will be caught up with them in the clouds to meet the Lord in the air. And so we will be with the Lord forever. (1 Thessalonians 4:16-17)

Are you listening for the trumpet blast? I am. Not that I think anyone will have to strain to hear it. There's not a person alive (or dead) who won't hear it. Of course, as is true when there's any loud, sudden noise, there will be an element of surprise when the trumpet blasts. For some, it will be a surprise full of terror and regret. For others, it will be a surprise of unimaginable joy.

Alas for that day! For the day of the LORD is near; it will come like destruction from the Almighty. Blow the trumpet in Zion; sound the alarm on My holy hill. Let all who live in the land tremble, for the day of the LORD is coming. It is close at hand... (Joel 1:15, 2:1)

Peter tells us,

But the day of the Lord will come like a thief. The heavens will disappear with a roar; the elements will be destroyed by fire, and the earth and everything in it will be laid bare. Since everything will be destroyed in this way, what kind of people ought you to be? You ought to

live holy and godly lives as you look forward
to the day of God and speed its coming. (2
Peter 3:10-12)

What will this day bring to you? Terror or exhilaration?
If you're not sure, you need to turn away from your sins and
surrender your life to Yeshua. You can do it with a simple
prayer right now, wherever you are.

Just tell God, in your own words, that you realize you
are a sinner and, as such, deserving of punishment. Tell Him
that you want to accept the sacrifice of Yeshua, who paid the
penalty for your sins when He was crucified in your behalf.
Ask Him to forgive you, cleanse you, and help you to walk in
righteousness for the rest of your days.

A simple, sincere prayer will open the gates of heaven
to any man, woman or child, regardless of the sins they may
have committed. God's grace is freely available to all who ask.
And, once you have stepped into His grace, you will be ready
for the trumpet blast that is about to shake the entire world.

A friend of mine likes to tell a story about something
that happened when he was attending college in southern
California. He came out of the library late one night, looked
up, and saw what appeared to be a ball of fire in the sky.

Whatever it was, it seemed to be bigger than the noon-
day sun, and it was growing. Daylight seemed to be growing
in the night sky. He looked around and saw that other stu-
dents also stood transfixed, their eyes focused on the sky.

My friend immediately began remembering Bible verses he'd learned as a child, about strange signs in the sky that would herald the Second Coming. His heart pounded as he wondered if he was witnessing the moment of Jesus' return — and he realized that he was not ready to meet the Lord.

Of course, as it turned out, that wasn't what was happening.

He found out later that a test rocket had been fired from nearby Vandenberg Air Force Base. Somehow, the rocket had gone off course, and had been destroyed over Los Angeles, causing a massive explosion in the upper atmosphere that kept the sky glowing for several minutes. Although the event wasn't supernatural in origin, it did have a deep impact on my friend, who made the decision right then to live for Jesus. He wanted to be sure he was ready the next time he saw a great light in the sky or heard the sound of a trumpet's blast.

Again, let me ask the question: *Are you ready?*

Yom Kippur

Yom Kippur is the holiest day of the Jewish Year. Whereas all the other Festivals are to be joyous occasions with eating, singing and dancing before the Lord, Yom Kippur is a solemn time of acknowledging sins and seeking God's forgiveness and mercy.

Yom Kippur, also known as the Day of Atonement, was the only time of the year the High Priest could enter the Most Holy Place of the Temple to atone for his own sins, as well as for the sins of his family and the entire Nation. This was done by sacrificing a bull and a goat and sprinkling the blood of these animals on the mercy seat.

It was also on this day that a scapegoat was brought to the leaders of Israel. They would lay hands on the animal, symbolically placing the sins of the Nation on it. Then it was driven into the wilderness, carrying the Nation's sins with it.

Why were there two goats? The first one was to atone (pay) for the People's sins. The second was to remove those sins from their presence. The blood of the first goat brought forgiveness. The second goat brought cleansing and righteousness.

But only for a short while. By the time another year went by and the next Day of Atonement came around, the People were once again covered with the filth and grime of their sinful nature and desperately in need of another sacrifice.

Yom Kippur looks forward to the day prophesied by Isaiah, when *the Redeemer will come to Zion, to those in Jacob who repent of their sins.* (Isaiah 59:20) Isaiah anticipated the Yom Kippur to end all Yom Kippurs. On that day the sins of Israel will be forgiven forever, and there will be no further need for the blood of bulls and goats, or a scapegoat.

I believe with my entire being that this day is almost here. The People of Israel — and, in fact, the people of every nation, tribe and culture — will come face to face with the Lord Yeshua Himself. Jesus is our High Priest, the sacrifice for the atonement of our sins, and our scapegoat — all three in one.

The author of Hebrews explains that,

> Christ did not enter a man-made sanctuary that was only a copy of the true one; He entered heaven itself, now to appear for us in God's presence. (Hebrews 9:24)

Hebrews goes on to explain that Jesus did not have to make a yearly sacrifice, as the High Priest did, *with blood that is not his own.* Instead,

> Christ was sacrificed once to take away the sins of many people; and He will appear a second time, not to bear sin, but to bring salvation to those who are waiting for Him. (Hebrews 9:28)

One day very soon, Yeshua HaMashiach, (Jesus the Messiah), will return to earth, bringing lasting peace and freedom from the effects of sin to all who have accepted His sacrifice.

Sukkot

The third and final feast that will see its fulfillment in Messiah's return is Sukkot, otherwise known as the Feast of Tabernacles, the Feast of Ingathering, or the Feast of Booths. Sukkot, which begins five days after Yom Kippur is a seven-day period during which the Jewish People remember God's faithfulness and provision through their 40-year period of wandering in the wilderness.

Specifically, they recall how God supplied the Children of Israel during the 40 years in the wilderness with food, water, shelter, clothing, guidance, light, and heat. During the week of Sukkot, each Jewish family lives in a small temporary dwelling made of branches. At night, they look up at the stars and remember God's promise to Abraham that his descendants would be as numerous as the stars in the heavens.

There are so many ways this festival points to Yeshua.

First, just as God gave the Israelites manna and water in the wilderness, Yeshua is spiritual bread and water for all who believe in Him. He said,

> "I am the bread of life. He who comes to Me will never go hungry, and he who believes in Me will never be thirsty." (John 6:35)

Paul even says that the Israelites

> ... drank from the spiritual rock that accompanied them; and that rock was [Yeshua]. (1 Corinthians 10:4)

Jesus Himself proclaimed,

> "I am the bread of life. Your forefathers ate the manna in the desert, yet they died. But here is the bread that comes down

from heaven, which a man may eat and not die. I am the living bread that came down from heaven. If anyone eats of this bread, he will live forever. This bread is My flesh, which I give for the life of the world." (John 6:48-51)

Every day during Sukkot, a water ceremony called *Nisuach HaMayim* was carried out, during which the High Priest and his assistant would draw water from the Pool of Siloam and pour out water and wine onto the altar of the Temple as the People sang, *with joy you will draw water from the wells of salvation.* (Isaiah 12:3)

It was most likely during this time that Yeshua stood up and cried out in a loud voice,

> "If anyone is thirsty, let him come to Me and drink. Whoever believes in Me, as the Scripture has said, streams of living water will flow from within him." (John 7:37-38)

Yeshua is the bread, the water, the light (John 8:12), and the Man whose name is the Branch. (Zechariah 6:12) In short, Sukkot is all about Him.

Speaking to the Prophet Zechariah, God said, *Take the silver and gold and make a crown, and set it on the head of the High Priest, Joshua...* (Zechariah 6:11.)

He also said:

> "Here is the man whose name is the Branch, and He will branch out from His place and build the temple of the LORD. It is He who will build the temple of the LORD, and He will be clothed with majesty and will sit and rule on His throne. And He will be a priest on His throne. And there will be harmony between the two." (Zechariah 6:12-13)

God also allowed the Prophet Jeremiah to foresee this day:

> "In those days and at that time I will make a righteous Branch sprout from David's line; He will do what is just and right in the land. In those days Judah will be saved and Jerusalem will live in safety. This is the name by which it will be called: The LORD Our Righteousness." (Jeremiah 33:15-16)

Obviously, these prophets were looking toward the day when the Messiah takes His throne in Jerusalem and assumes His rightful position as Priest and King. I'm convinced this wonderful and glorious day is almost here.

It amazes me to think that every year, millions of Jews all over the world celebrate holy days that point so clearly to

Yeshua, and yet they don't really understand the significance of what they're doing.

For some, the light is about to come on, flooding their lives and hearts with joy.

Part Three

A FEW FINAL WORDS

Chapter Twelve

THE WORLD'S DEBT TO THE JEWS

In the 12th chapter of Genesis, God promised Abraham that *I will bless those who bless you and curse those who curse you.* He also promised that all nations would be blessed through Abraham's seed. That promise was fulfilled through the birth, life, death and resurrection of Yeshua.

But there are many other ways the world has been blessed through the Jewish People.

For example, have you ever heard of a fellow by the name of Albert Einstein?

He was a Jew.

How about Robert Oppenheimer, the rocket scientist?

Jewish.

The two men who conquered polio — Jonas Salk and Albert Sabin?

That's right. Both were Jews.

In fact, although Jews make up only .2% of the world's population, Jews have won 23 percent of the Nobel Prizes since the award was established in 1901.

Jews have been responsible for great advancements in medicine, science, literature and culture. The Jewish People have truly been a blessing to the world.

This is just one more way God's promise to Abraham, given in the twelfth chapter of Genesis, that *all peoples on earth will be blessed through you* has come true.

Will you allow me just a few moments of Jewish pride? Let me tell you just some of what Abraham's children have given to the world. Jews:

- Discovered insulin. (Dr. Frederick Banting)
- First used aspirin for relieving pain. (Felix Hoffmann)
- Discovered and calculated the speed of light. (Galileo)
- Identified the first cancer virus. (Briton Epstein)
- Discovered how infectious diseases spread (so they could be stopped from spreading). (Baruch Blumberg)
- Developed streptomycin, and coined the word "antibiotic." (Selman Waksman)
- Invented color photography. (Gabriel Lipmann)
- Discovered the law of thermodynamics. (Julius Mayer)

Jews gave the world blue jeans, the sewing machine, and, according to many historians, discovered America. That's right, Christopher Columbus was most likely Jewish.

Ever heard of an organization called The American Red Cross? It was founded by a Jew, Adolphus Simeon Solomons. In the 1880s, he held a number of meetings in his home in Washington, D.C., to discuss the founding and incorporation of the organization. Solomons was so highly regarded that he was asked to stand in for Vice President Schuyler Colfax when Colfax was unable to speak at the dedication of a brand-new YMCA in Washington.

When you look at all the things Jewish People have contributed to society, it adds a new dimension of horror to the Holocaust. Just think of all the discoveries, inventions and other contributions that were lost to the world forever because of Hitler's murderous hatred of the Jews.

That reminds me of a passage in the book of Sanhedrin in the Talmud: *We find in the case of Cain, who killed his brother, that it is written: The bloods of thy brother cry unto me: not the blood of thy brother, but the bloods of thy brother is said, that is, his blood and the blood of his potential descendants.* [29]

I don't mean to boast. I can't take an iota of credit for anything anyone else has done. But it does make my heart swell with pride when I think of all the ways God has blessed the world through my People. It also shows me that unreasoning hatred of Jews, the tendency on the part of some to blame the Jews for everything that goes wrong in the world (as Hitler did) is complete lunacy. It has absolutely no basis in fact.

Here are just a few more of the ways Abraham's descendants have blessed the world.

Music

After 9-11, *God Bless America* became one of our country's favorite songs. You heard it everywhere, most especially at sporting events. The song, first made popular by Kate Smith way back in 1939, was played during the seventh-inning stretch throughout Major League Baseball's playoffs and the world series. The song was written by a Jew, **Irving Berlin**, whose family fled to America to escape pogroms that were taking place in Russia. Berlin also wrote the song that became the best-selling record of all time, *White Christmas.* Altogether, he wrote more than 900 songs, including *There's No Business Like Show Business* and *Easter Parade.*

And if those aren't your favorite tunes, how do you feel about *Rhapsody in Blue?* That, too, was written by a Jew, **George Gershwin**.

Want more?

How about **Bob Dylan**? He, too, is Jewish. (I realize that I should have mentioned **Benny Goodman, Beverly Sills, Barbra Streisand, Leonard Bernstein, Stephen Sondheim**, and maybe even **Neil Diamond** and **Barry Manilow** — and the list goes on...)

Literature

If you like science fiction, or just about any other kind of book, you certainly know the name of **Isaac Asimov.** Asimov was undoubtedly one of the most prolific writers of all time, having written or edited more than 500 books on all types of subjects. Can you imagine? That's one book a month for more than 40 years! Asimov's literary works have been published in nine of the ten major categories of the Dewey Decimal System. Philosophy is the only category that doesn't have at least one Asimov book.

Other Jews who have contributed much to the world of books include Nobel Laureate **Isaac Beshavis Singer, Boris Pasternak, Chaim Potok, Saul Bellow, Arthur Miller, E.L. Doctorow** and two of my favorite children's writers — **Maurice Sendak** and **Shel Silverstein.**

Laughter

Do you like to laugh? Who doesn't? Laughter is one of God's great gifts to His people. The Bible says, *A cheerful heart is good medicine...* (Proverbs 17:22) And in recent times, medical science has shown this is true.

Many Jews have blessed the world in this way. Here are just a few:

- **Woody Allen**
- **Jack Benny**
- **Milton Berle**
- **Victor Borge**
- **Albert Brooks**
- **Mel Brooks**
- **George Burns**
- **Sid Caesar**
- **Billy Crystal**
- **Buddy Hackett**
- **Danny Kaye**
- **Alan King**
- **Jerry Lewis**

- **The Marx Brothers**
- **Adam Sandler**
- **Jerry Seinfeld**
- **Peter Sellers**
- **Phil Silvers**
- **Ben Stiller**
- **Henny Youngman**

Sports

Maybe sports isn't all that important compared to things like medicine, physics, music and literature. Then again, sports is a gift from God, and I wouldn't be a bit surprised to find out that there are a whole lot of excellent softball leagues in Heaven. (And if you're a golfer, can't you just imagine playing 18-holes in Paradise?)

Besides, when the conversation turns to great sports heroes, there aren't very many Jews who come to mind, right? Well, just off the top of my head, I can think of three Jewish stars who were among the greatest their sports ever saw.

The first, is **Sandy Koufax,** arguably the greatest pitcher major league baseball has ever seen. If an arm injury hadn't forced Koufax to retire at 27, there's no telling how many games he would have won. As it was, he threw four no-hitters, earned 27 victories during the final year of his career, and was elected to baseball's Hall of Fame on the first ballot. Koufax is also remembered for sitting out a World Series game in 1965 because it was scheduled on Yom Kippur.

Hank Greenberg was another great baseball hero. In 1937, Greenberg had an incredible 183 runs batted in, one short of the American League record set by the Yankees' Lou Gehrig. The following year, he nearly broke Babe Ruth's single season home run record, winding up with 58. In 1941, when Greenberg was the highest paid player in major league baseball, he was drafted into the army. He was discharged just prior to the bombing of Pearl Harbor because of a new government policy to release soldiers who were older than 28. Greenberg immediately re-enlisted. For the next four years, he served in the Army Air Force and saw action in the China-India-Burma Theater. Greenberg returned to baseball in the middle of the 1945 season. The following year, he led the league with 44 homeruns.

And how about **Mark Spitz?** All he did was win seven gold medals in swimming and set a new world record in every event he entered at the 1972 Olympics in Munich. That was the year when 11 members of the Israeli Olympic team were murdered by terrorists. Spitz himself was surrounded with bodyguards throughout the Olympics, since it was thought, with good reason, that he too could be a terrorist target.

Nevertheless, he went on to capture gold medals, and set records, in the 100-meter freestyle, 200-meter freestyle, 100-meter butterfly, 200-meter butterfly, the 100-meter freestyle relay, the 200-meter freestyle relay, and the 100-meter medley relay. Altogether, Mark Spitz won nine Olympic medals, making him one of only four athletes to ever accomplish that feat.

Space Flight

Judith Resnik, the second woman into outer space, was also a Jew. Tragically, she lost her life when the Space Shuttle Challenger exploded during its launch on January 28, 1986.

Resnik, who held a doctorate in electrical engineering and played classical piano, was selected for the astronaut program in 1978 at the age of 27. She served as a mission specialist on the first voyage of the Discovery in August of 1984.

Ilan Ramon, the first Israeli in outer space aboard the U.S. Space Shuttle Columbia, was an Israeli fighter pilot, child of Holocaust survivors, and father of four. He saw his voyage as much more than a science expedition. He believed he was on a higher mission *as an ambassador representing all Jews and Israelis.* Ramon was selected to represent Israel based on his air force training and science education. As a combat pilot, he fought in the 1973 Yom Kippur War, and in Lebanon in 1982 where he survived a collision and ejected from his fighter jet. Ramon is a recipient of the Congressional Space Medal of Honor. He and his six crew members did not survive an accident upon re-entry of their mission.

Heroes in Battle

Frances Slanger, known as the *American Florence Nightingale*, was one of the first women ashore during the Allied Invasion of Normandy on D-Day, June 6, 1944.

As she waded to shore with the hospital platoon, bullets flying all around her, Nurse Slanger had to hold on to the belts of other soldiers to keep from being swept off her feet by the pounding waves.

Once on shore, she risked her life repeatedly to care for the wounded soldiers all around her. Slanger survived the carnage of Normandy and eventually made her way to France.

On October 21, 1944, she read an article in *The Stars and Stripes,* the newspaper for American soldiers, praising nurses like her for their heroism and hard work. Embarrassed, she pulled out a flashlight and wrote a letter to the paper:

> The GIs say we rough it, but we in our little tent can't see it. We wade ankle deep in mud. You have to lie in it. We have a stove and coal. We even have a laundry line in the tent... Sure we rough it. But you, the men behind the guns, driving our tanks, flying our planes, sailing our ships, building our bridges and the men who pave the way and the men who were left behind... it is to you we doff our helmets. To every GI wearing the American uniform, for you we have the greatest admiration and respect. [30]

An hour after writing that letter, Frances Slanger was killed by fragments of an exploding German artillery shell. She was buried in a military cemetery in France. The Star of David engraved on her tombstone told the world she was a Jew who died fighting for her country.

And she wasn't the only one.

More than 550,000 Jews served in America's armed forces during World War II. Nearly 11,000 gave their lives for their country and more than 40,000 were wounded. Two Jews received the Congressional Medal of Honor, 157 were awarded the Distinguished Service Medal and Crosses, and another 1,600 received the Silver Star.

Fighting Poverty

Rebecca Gratz, who was born in Philadelphia in 1781, is considered by many to be the mother of charitable causes within the United States. Some call her the *Mother Teresa* of her day.

Although Rebecca was born into a wealthy and socially connected family, she chose to dedicate her life to serving the less fortunate.

When she was only 20, Rebecca organized the Female Association for the Relief of Women and Children of Reduced Circumstances in Philadelphia. She also helped found the Philadelphia Orphan Asylum in 1815, and served as the organization's secretary for more than 40 years. Although most of her efforts helped people of all faiths and backgrounds, she also founded the Female Hebrew Benevolent Society and the Jewish Foster Home and Orphanage.

Thousands of needy men, women and children benefited from her selfless compassion and generosity.

The same can by said of **Nathan Straus**, who, in 1888, became one of the owners of R.H. Macy and company. At

Macy's Department Store in New York City, he was responsible for a number of important innovations, including health care and a lunchroom for his employees. He also had restrooms installed in the store.

Despite his business success, Straus never became a wealthy man. That's because he cared more about helping people than making money. In the bitterly cold winter of 1892-93, he distributed food to the poor and sold 1.5 million buckets of coal for five cents each. The following winter, he gave away more than $50,000 worth of coal, food and lodging. He also established lodging houses that provided bed and breakfast for five cents.

If I tried to list all of the Jews who've made contributions to America and the world, I'd be sure to leave out someone important. But before I leave this subject behind, let me list just a few more important Jews you may not know about — or that you may not have known were Jews.

Some of these people have been devout Jews, while others are not the least bit interested in God. Some have led exemplary lives, and some have been moral shipwrecks. But all have blessed the world in some way, and so have had a part in fulfilling God's promise to Abraham that *all peoples on earth will be blessed through you.*

Why am I going on about all of the contributions these Jews have made to our society? Because I want to emphasize that there are many great and honorable Jewish People. And yet, the majority of them are completely and hopelessly lost. We must redouble our efforts to reach them with the Gospel. We can't let them die without Jesus. We can't let them be counted among God's enemies when the final trumpet sounds.

Did you know that all of these people were or are Jews?

- **Benjamin Disraeli,** twice British Prime Minister.
- **Kirk** and **Michael Douglas,** popular actors.
- **Richard Dreyfus,** Academy Award winning actor.
- **Peter Falk,** actor known best for his role as TV's *Columbo*.
- **Harrison Ford,** actor who portrayed Indiana Jones and Han Solo.
- **Kenny G.,** saxophonist who has sold millions of records all over the world.
- **Cary Grant,** one of film's great stars in the 1950s and 1960s.
- **Murray Gell-Mann,** Nobel Prize winning physicist who discovered the sub-atomic particles known as quarks.
- **Jascha Heifetz,** hailed as the greatest violinist of the 20th century.
- **William Herschel,** astronomer who discovered the planet Uranus.
- **Dustin Hoffman,** Academy Award winning actor.
- **Michael Landon,** beloved actor and producer, best known for his *Little House on the Prairie*.
- **Daniel Day-Lewis,** 2008 Best Actor Oscar winner.
- **Lise Meitner,** discoverer of nuclear fission.

- **Paul Newman,** another Academy Award winning actor, well-known as a philanthropist.
- **Gwyneth Paltrow,** Academy Award winning British actress.
- **Itzhak Perlman,** Grammy Award winning violinist.
- **Artie Shaw,** renowned bandleader.
- **William James Sidis,** considered by many to be the smartest man who ever lived, with an IQ of 250-300.
- **Isaac Stern,** another great violinist.
- **Noah Wyle,** actor on TV's *ER*.

There you have it. Just a few of the many ways God has blessed the world through the Jewish People.

But the best is yet to come.

Chapter Thirteen

THE BEST IS YET TO COME

Do you ever wake up in the middle of the night, and lie there listening to the silence?

Maybe you hear some crickets chirping outside your bedroom window. The ticking of your old-fashioned alarm clock. The deep breathing (or even snoring) of your mate.

But do you ever try to listen beyond the normal noises of daily life?

Could that be the first sound of a trumpet blast?

Is that an angelic choir?

Do I hear a mighty shout?

Does your heart ever start pounding with anticipation that the End of the Age could come at any moment?

When you get out of bed in the morning, do you ever think, *This could be my last day on earth?* When a car alarm goes off, do you ever think that it might be more than just a car alarm?

The truth is that all of us who belong to Messiah could go zooming up and out of this planet to meet the Lord in the air at any time. And I believe God wants us to live in expectation of that moment. Always listening. Always watching. Always expecting.

Jesus told us that His return will catch the world by surprise, like *a thief in the night*. He will come when the world least expects Him to. Those who love Him won't be caught off guard because they are looking for Him at all times.

> "As it was in the days of Noah, so it will be at the coming of the Son of Man. For in the days before the flood, people were eating and drinking, marrying and giving in marriage, up to the day Noah entered the ark; and they knew nothing about what would happen until the flood came and took them all away. That is how it will be at the coming of the Son of Man." (Matthew 24:37-39)

I know some believers who are worried that the world could end tomorrow. Some worry because they have loved ones who haven't committed themselves to Yeshua. I understand that fear because eternal salvation only comes through faith in Yeshua. And it is devastating to think that people you love will miss out on the joys of Heaven, simply because they've never said *yes* to the Messiah.

But other than that, I can't think of any reason why anyone who believes in Yeshua should be worried or distressed that the end is near. To me, that's like a player on a football team about to win the Super Bowl being worried because the game clock is winding down. It just doesn't make sense. Our eternal victory is about to be won! Our planet is going to be transformed!

Think about it.

It will be a world where the lion lies down with the lamb.

Nothing will hurt or destroy, and the whole earth will be full of the knowledge of the Lord.

God Himself will wipe the tears from the eyes of His People.

Who is the antichrist? It doesn't really matter to you. Just keep your eyes on Yeshua.

What is the mark of the beast? Again, as long as you have your eyes on the Lord, there is no reason at all for you to worry about such things.

If you belong to Jesus, you won't have to go through the times of war and tribulation about to come upon this planet. You and I will be rejoicing before God's throne, waiting until the time is right for us to return with Yeshua to serve as judges and rulers in the new earth.

The Rapture is coming

Terrible times are on their way for Planet Earth. War. Drought. Pestilence. A dictator so evil that he will make Hitler seem like *an ordinary guy* by comparison.

But again, if you belong to Yeshua, you won't be here on earth to experience any of these catastrophes.

I just quoted from the 24th chapter of Matthew, where Jesus talks about what will be happening here on earth when He returns. In the next three verses, He says:

"Two men will be in the field; one will be taken and the other left. Two women will be grinding with a hand mill; one will be taken and the other left. Therefore keep watch, because you do not know on what day your Lord will come." (Matthew 24:40-42)

Jesus is talking about the Rapture, when we believers will rise into the air to meet our Messiah and begin our eternal lives in the glory of Heaven. I don't know exactly how the Rapture will occur. Some theologians believe we will rise into the air physically. Others have come to the conclusion that we will simply leave our bodies behind, leaving those who remain on earth to contemplate the *sudden plague* that has killed so many men, women and children.

The Apostle Paul wrote to the Thessalonians:

We believe that Jesus died and rose again and so we believe that God will bring with Jesus those who have fallen asleep in Him. According to the Lord's own word, we tell you that we who are still alive, who are left till the coming of the Lord, will certainly not precede those who have fallen asleep. For the Lord Himself will come down from heaven, with a loud command, with the voice of the archangel and with the trumpet call of God, and the dead in Christ will rise first. After that, we who are still alive and are left will be caught up together with them in the clouds to meet the Lord in the air. And so we will be with the Lord forever. Therefore encourage each other with these words. (1 Thessalonians 4:14-18)

He also told the believers at Corinth,

Listen, I tell you a mystery: We will not all sleep, but we will all be changed — in a flash, in the twinkling of an eye, at the last trumpet. For the trumpet will sound, the dead will be raised imperishable, and we will be changed. (1 Corinthians 15:51-52)

Although this will be the end of life on earth, as we know it, this planet will continue to spin through space for a few more years — painful, difficult years.

A world of woe

The Book of Revelation paints a vivid picture of the suffering that will take place during this time. It seems clear to me that the antichrist will unleash nuclear weapons in his battle to set up a one-world government, and it may be that the worldwide famine, *bitter water* and other deadly calamities prophesied by the Apostle John will come as a result of radiation and nuclear fallout. It makes sense.

But whether or not this is the case, John writes, *A third of mankind was killed by the three plagues of fire, smoke and sulfur.* (Revelation 9:18)

Despite the terror that will grip the earth at that time, there will be a great spiritual revival. Millions who were left behind during the Rapture will recognize the error of their ways and call out to Yeshua to save them. Many will be martyred for their faith. Others will die in battle against satan's forces.

But in the end, God's people will prevail, the earth will be cleansed of evil, and Yeshua will sit down on His throne in Jerusalem to begin His 1,000 year reign.

For the very first time since the days of Adam and Eve, we will experience God's creation the way it was meant to be.

Imagine knowing that the Messiah Himself is literally on the throne in Jerusalem. Can you imagine how thrilling it will be to travel to Jerusalem for an audience with The King Himself? Think of the happy tears you'll cry when you're reunited with believing loved ones who were taken from you by death? Imagine knowing that the world is free from corruption, violence, and greed. Can you envision living in a world where there are no hungry children, where no one is homeless, where no country has rockets aimed at another, where there is no need to fear terrorist strikes of any kind? There will be no scientists working feverishly to find the cure for a disease, because there will be no disease.

What an absolutely glorious time it will be!

This is where my story ends. I will leave it to others to dissect the Book of Revelation, figure out the identity of the antichrist, and provide a chronology of battles and other events. As I said when we started this journey together, this is not my purpose in writing this book.

Before we close, I want to recap the **Six Reasons** why I am certain the Last Days are upon us:

1. Anti-Semitism is on the rise around the world.
2. Scattered Jews are returning to Israel in record numbers.
3. Increasing numbers of Jews are accepting Yeshua as Messiah, as the blinders are removed from their eyes.
4. The Gospel is being preached to the nations.
5. The stage is set for the Messiah's return.
6. The times of the Gentiles are coming to an end.

Yeshua is coming soon. Are you ready for His return?

The most important thing you can ever do is accept His sacrifice on your behalf and recognize Him as the Messiah of Israel and the world and the Lord of your life. If you haven't already done this, you can do it right now. All it takes is a simple, sincere, heartfelt prayer. You can use the following if you'd like — or put it into your own words:

> Lord Yeshua, I acknowledge You as Messiah and Savior of my soul. I know that I am a sinner, worthy of death and eternal separation from God. I know that You paid the penalty for my sins when You were crucified on the cross, and believe You were resurrected from

the dead on the third day. I ask You to cleanse me through Your blood and save my soul. In Your holy name I pray, Amen.

If you prayed that prayer, congratulations! Your new life has begun, and you can look forward with joyful anticipation to Yeshua's return!

Before we close, I want to give a quick reminder of some other actions you can take to help prepare for Messiah's return. You can:

Pray for the Jewish People to come to know their Messiah

Ask God to give you His heart of love and compassion for His People. Ask Him to give you a burden for their redemption. When you understand God's heart for the Jews, you will pray with passion and urgency, and many Jewish souls will be added to His Kingdom.

Support Messianic organizations that are helping Jews return to Israel

As we discussed earlier, you can help fulfill biblical prophecy by bringing Jews home to the Holy Land. Thousands of Jews from all over the world are returning to Israel, and this is a clear sign that the Last Days are upon us.

Study the Jewish roots of your faith

Do you know the history of your family? Where were your ancestors born? When did they come to America? What were your grandparents like? Over the last twenty years or so, many Americans have devoted much time and energy to uncovering the roots of their family tree.

But what about your spiritual roots? If you believe in Yeshua, your roots are Jewish. Every Christian ought to know something about Jewish culture and customs. You may want to learn about and observe the biblical feasts. Doing so will help you understand the Hebraic roots of your faith, and I believe it will also draw you closer to God.

Encourage support of Israel

Let your senators and congressmen know that you support Israel, and that you expect the United States to do the same. No government on earth is perfect, including Israel's Knesset. So I'm not saying we have to support every single move Israel makes. But I do think we need to be strong in our support of Israel's right to exist, and let it be known that we will never turn away from her or desert her to her enemies.

Talk to your Jewish friends about Yeshua

They may not want to hear what you have to say. They may become angry or even stand up and walk out on you.

But do it anyway.

Some who may be terribly angry with you right now, will thank you over and over again, throughout eternity, that you cared enough to tell them about their Savior's love.

Life from the dead is coming

Soon, life from the dead will be poured out on the world, *and God will wipe away every tear from their eyes...* the eyes of His People. (Revelation 7:17)

Are you ready?

Please don't miss out.

Tell Yeshua right now that you want to surrender your heart and your life to Him. He will hear you and respond, and your life will never be the same.

I leave you with these final words:

Listen and hear.

The trumpet is about to sound.

Footnotes

[1]   Time Magazine, December 1967

[2]   Quoted in www.avoiceinthewilderness.com

[3]   Quoted in www.avoiceinthewilderness.com

[4]   Quoted in www.avoiceinthewilderness.com

[5]   Quoted in www.adl.org

[6]   Quoted in www.cnn.com, October 27, 2005

[7]   Quoted in www.cnn.com, February 5, 2002

[8]   Brown, Dr. Michael: *Our Hands Are Stained with Blood;* Shippensburg, PA; Destiny Image Publishers, 1990

[9]   Katz, Nathan and Goldberg, Ellen S., article titled "The Last Jews in India and Burma," published by Jerusalem Center for Public Affairs, April 15, 1988

[10]   Schneider, Ludwig article titled, "Blind to Biblical Prophecy," published in Israel Today, August 2, 2007.

[11]   Martyr, Justin *The Dialogue with Trypho*, translated by A. Lukyn Williams, S.P.C.K., London, 1930, P.169, Sec. 80.1-5

[12]   Gruber, Daniel: *The Church and the Jews, the Biblical Relationship;* Springfield, MO, General Council of the Assemblies of God, International Ministries, 1991

[13]   Thoma, Gary article in Christianity Today, September 7, 1998, "The Return of the Jewish Church."

14   Teplinsky, Sandra: *Out of the Darkness;* Jacksonville
      Beach, FL: Hear O Israel Publishing, 1998, Pages 44-45

15   Glasser, Arthur F., Fuller Theological Seminary News
      Release, May 12, 1976

16   "The Thailand Report on Jewish People," Occasional
      Paper #7, issued in 1980 by the Lausanne Committee
      for World Evangelization

17   *Babylonian Talmud,* Sanhedrin 98a

18   McDowell, Josh: *The New Evidence That Demands a
      Verdict;* Nashville, TN, Thomas Nelson Publishers, 1999

19   JewishEncyclopedia.com, Shabbethaai Zebi B. Mordecai,
      article by Kaufmann Kohler and Henry Malter

20   Article in Christianity Today, *the Return of the Jewish
      Church,* by Gary Thoma, September 7, 1998

21   From Israel Ministry of Foreign Affairs website,
      www.mfa.gov.il

22   Quote from www.sixdaywar.org

23   From sixdaywar.org

24   From sixdaywar.org

25   From sixdaywar.org

26   Creators Syndicate column by Dennis Prager, "Those
      who curse the Jews and those who bless the Jews," 2008

27   Koenig, Bill: *Eye to Eye — Facing the Consequences of
      Dividing Israel;* Springfield, MO, 21st Century Press, 2004

28   Eckstein, Yechiel: The Journey Home, Shavti House, 2001

29   *Babylonian Talmud,* Sanhedrin 98a

30   Slanger, Francis: "Jewish Heroes and Heroines in
      America," www.fau.edu

Note: All scriptural references are taken from the New
International Version (NIV), International Bible Society, 1978,
unless otherwise noted in text.

About the Author

For more than 25 years, Jonathan Bernis, President and CEO of Jewish Voice Ministries International (JVMI), has worked on the forefront of world evangelism, taking the Good News of Israel's Messiah to the far reaches of the earth—to Israel, scattered among the nations, and also to the Gentiles.

A Messianic Rabbi, Jonathan founded *Shema Yisrael Messianic Congregation* in Rochester, NY in 1984, where he served as Senior Pastor for nearly a decade. As the walls of communism fell in the former Soviet Union, Jonathan answered the call of the Lord to bring the message of Yeshua (Jesus) to a land long held in darkness and oppression, producing the first large-scale festival outreach in St. Petersburg, Russia in May 1993. He was overwhelmed by the vast numbers of people hungry for Messiah ...*half of them Jewish!*

Hear O' Israel! Ministries was born—a unique outreach organization producing large-scale International Festivals of Jewish Music and Dance, sharing the Good News to eager audiences of Jews and Gentiles. Jonathan moved to St. Petersburg, Russia where he founded the *Messianic Center of St. Petersburg*, the first of many training centers worldwide, formed to equip and train a new generation of Jewish Believers for ministry in this ripe new field of harvest. Now known as *Messianic Jewish Bible Institutes* (MJBI), training centers have been established from Russia and Ukraine, to South America, Korea, the United States, and Ethiopia.

More than 500,000 people attended these vibrant festivals throughout Eastern Europe, India, Africa and South America. Millions more participated via live television broadcasts. Approximately one-third of the tens of thousands responding to altar calls were Jewish—*numbers not seen since the first century.* More than a dozen new Messianic Jewish congregations have been birthed in Russia and Ukraine through these outreaches.

When Jonathan merged *Hear O' Israel!* with *Jewish Voice Broadcasts* in 1999, it was a marriage of broadcast capability and large-scale regional outreach—a strategic partnership for the 21st century, expanding the scope and effectiveness of both ministries. In 2008, JVMI completed its state-of-the-art High Definition Messianic Media Center in Phoenix, with a soundstage capable of seating a live audience of more than 100 and producing network quality programs.

The mission of JVMI is two-fold; proclaim the Gospel to the Jew first, and also to the Nations (Romans 1:16), and equip the Church to reach the Jewish People—providing education about the Hebraic Roots of Christianity, the Church's responsibility to Israel and the Jewish People, and how to share the Messiah effectively with the Jewish People. The Good News is proclaimed through television, print media, large-scale international festivals, and humanitarian/medical outreaches.

The Lost Tribes of the House of Israel are of particular interest to Jonathan and JVMI. A prophetic sign of redemption, as God reveals these enigmatic peoples, scattered to the four corners of the earth, whether it be Ethiopia or the far reaches of Eastern India, JVMI reaches out with essential humanitarian and medical provision, as God's arm extended in the love of their Messiah. This is a very exciting and rewarding area of ministry, particularly close to Jonathan's heart, as these are the poorest Jewish communities on earth.

Jonathan hosts a weekly television program called *Jewish Voice with Jonathan Bernis*, which is aired throughout the United States, Canada, Europe, Asia and Israel. Unique among Christian broadcasting, *Jewish Voice with Jonathan Bernis* brings a distinctly Hebraic *voice* and view, with prophetic news from Israel and around the world, testimonies, and insights from international guests.

A much sought after speaker, Jonathan teaches at conferences and churches around the world. A passionate supporter of Israel, he is an active member on the board of several Israel-based and pro-Israel ministries, and has been instrumental in the founding and support of many pro-Israel and Israel/Church reconciliation organizations, including *Toward Jerusalem Council II, Road to Jerusalem, Maoz Israel,* and *Promise Keepers.*

Jonathan holds university degrees in Theology, Jewish Studies and Early Christianity, and has done extensive postgraduate study in archaeology, including work on archaeological excavations in Israel. He has led more than 30 teaching tours to Israel since 1984.

Jonathan resides in Phoenix, Arizona with his wife Elisangela, and their daughter, Li'el.

Other Publications By Jonathan Bernis:

- A Hope and a Future - Booklet or CD

- Chanukah, Feast of Dedication - Booklet

- The Expanding Kingdom - Booklet or CD

- The Feasts of Israel - CD

- God's Plan for Israel - CD

- Tasting the Bread of Life - CD

- The Dangerous Lie of Replacement Theology - CD

- The Role of Israel in Last Days Prophecy - CD

- 7 Keys to Unlocking the Prophetic Mysteries of Israel - Book

- Messianic Passover DVD & Haggadah Booklet

For more information:
www.jewishvoice.org